# SOLO Taxonom
# A Guide for Schools

**A common language of learning** — **Book 1**

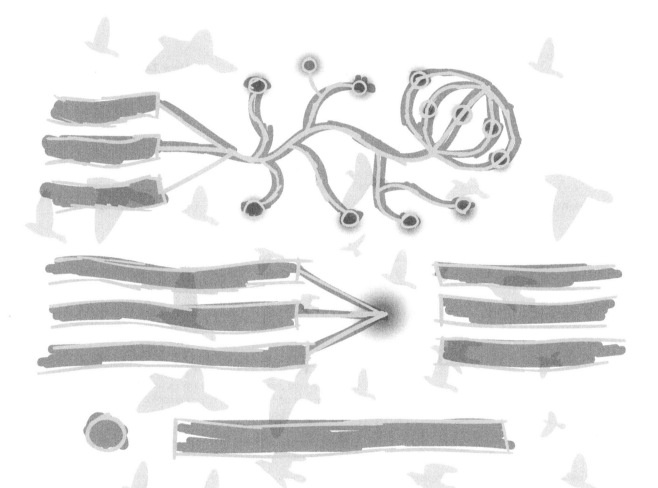

# Pam Hook and Julie Mills

GW01046102

**essential
resources**

| | |
|---|---|
| **Title:** | SOLO Taxonomy: A Guide for Schools<br>Book 1: A common language of learning |
| **Authors:** | Pam Hook and Julie Mills |
| **Editor:** | Tanya Tremewan |
| **Designer:** | Freshfields Graphic Design |
| **Book code:** | 5619 |
| **ISBN:** | 978-1-927143-56-8 |
| **Published:** | 2011 |
| **Publisher:** | Essential Resources Educational Publishers Limited |

| **United Kingdom:** | **Australia:** | **New Zealand:** |
|---|---|---|
| Units 8–10 Parkside | PO Box 906 | PO Box 5036 |
| Shortgate Lane | Strawberry Hills | Invercargill |
| Laughton BN8 6DG | NSW 2012 | |
| ph: 0845 3636 147 | ph: 1800 005 068 | ph: 0800 087 376 |
| fax: 0845 3636 148 | fax: 1800 981 213 | fax: 0800 937 825 |

| | |
|---|---|
| **Websites:** | www.essentialresourcesuk.com<br>www.essentialresources.com.au<br>www.essentialresources.co.nz |
| **Copyright:** | Text: © Pam Hook and Julie Mills, 2011<br>Edition and illustrations:<br>© Essential Resources Educational Publishers Limited, 2011 |

**About the authors:** Pam Hook is an educational consultant (Hooked on Thinking), who works with New Zealand schools to develop curricula and pedagogies for learning to learn based on SOLO Taxonomy. She has published articles on thinking, learning, e-learning and gifted education, writes curriculum material for government and business, directs Ministry of Education e-learning contracts and is co-author of two science textbooks widely used in New Zealand secondary schools. She is known for her educational blog (http://artichoke.typepad.com) and is a popular keynote speaker at conferences.

Julie Mills has been an educational consultant in learning and teaching since 2005, working in schools throughout New Zealand with a focus on raising student achievement. With a depth of understanding of curriculum, achievement and assessment practices, she facilitates a range of contracts for the Ministry of Education and writes educational resources for both the public and private sectors. She presents regularly at conferences as well as working closely with principals/ headteachers who are initiating change in schools. Julie has an extensive background in teaching at all primary and intermediate levels. She has also held senior management positions and was a founding school principal for four years.

**Acknowledgements:** Thanks to Professor John Biggs for his encouragement and ongoing critique of our work using SOLO Taxonomy and to the many New Zealand teachers and schools who have introduced SOLO Taxonomy as a common language of learning outcomes to their students. We are also grateful to the New Zealand schools that provided examples of student learning outcomes for the book: Halsey Drive School, Jean Batten School, St Thomas's School, Lincoln High School, Newmarket Primary School, Northcross Intermediate School, Onehunga Primary School, Our Lady Star of the Sea School, Sunset Primary School and Waterlea Primary School.

# Contents

Introduction    4

## 1. Introducing SOLO Taxonomy    5

What is SOLO Taxonomy?    5

Why is SOLO Taxonomy useful?    10

## 2. How can schools, teachers and students use SOLO Taxonomy?    11

SOLO on display – talking about and seeing SOLO levels in all learning areas    11

SOLO learning verbs – a common language of learning    13

Constructive alignment    14

Designing three-level "assessment for learning" tasks    17

Student learning logs    20

## 3. Effective strategies and success criteria    22

What are HOT SOLO maps?    22

How do HOT SOLO maps work together with target vocabulary and self assessment rubrics?    22

What are the benefits of this approach?    28

Overview of HOT SOLO maps    29

Unistructural and multistructural HOT SOLO maps    30

Relational HOT SOLO maps    36

Extended abstract HOT SOLO maps    54

## 4. Where to next?    63

References    63

Index of templates    64

# Introduction

*SOLO Taxonomy: A Guide for Schools* is a series designed to help teachers and schools implement a common understanding and language of learning that will help students "learn how to learn". At its heart is SOLO Taxonomy, a model developed by John Biggs and Kevin Collis which has proven its value to teachers and students at all primary and secondary levels. Guided by this series, you can realise the many benefits of SOLO Taxonomy, such as its capacity to make learning outcomes visible, identify their level of cognitive complexity, and consequently make feedback and "feed forward" more effective in the learning process.

A focus of this first book in the series is to help teachers and principals to harness SOLO Taxonomy to use a common language of learning, and in particular to:

- use SOLO verbs to write learning intentions for achievement objectives and achievement standards (constructive alignment)
- identify effective strategies and success criteria to support these learning intentions (HOT SOLO maps and self assessment rubrics).

A second major focus is to help students self assess their learning outcomes with three-level "assessment for learning" tasks and learning logs.

The four sections take you through the effective process of developing a common language of learning across a school:

1. **Introducing SOLO Taxonomy** outlines the essential features of this innovative model of learning and summarises why it is useful.

2. **How can schools, teachers and students use SOLO Taxonomy?** sets out ideas and templates for implementing and communicating about the model at both whole-school and class levels.

3. **Effective strategies and success criteria** provides guidance for using HOT SOLO maps, target vocabulary and self assessment rubrics, along with relevant templates.

4. **Where to next?** introduces planning learning experiences as the important next step in the learning process with SOLO Taxonomy.

At the back of this book is an index for easy access to all of the templates set out in this book.

# 1. Introducing SOLO Taxonomy

*Before we knew about SOLO we were basically prestructural or unistructural [about learning;] we didn't know how to get up to relational or extended abstract. Learning was just ... you know ... ask a question and answer it. But now we can get deeper and find out more using this thinking. It is definitely better now we know what to do.*

Year 4 students describe learning with SOLO Taxonomy (Hook, in press)

An important step in helping students "learn how to learn" is taken when teachers and students clarify their understanding of learning beyond metaphors like "learning is a narrative" and "learning is a journey". *SOLO Taxonomy: A Guide for Schools* offers a surefooted way to take this step.

The Structure of Observed Learning Outcomes (SOLO) Taxonomy developed by Biggs and Collis (1982) is a model of learning outcomes that helps schools develop a common understanding and language of learning and in so doing helps teachers and students to understand the learning process and learning outcomes. With SOLO Taxonomy, teachers and students are able to:

- thoughtfully design learning intentions and learning experiences
- identify and use effective strategies and success criteria
- provide feedback and feed forward assessment of learning outcomes
- reflect meaningfully on what to do next.

The simple argument holds that teachers who adopt constructivist learning theories have different understandings of learning from teachers who take a behaviourist approach. The former are likely to think of themselves as facilitators of learning in the classroom, "guides on the side" providing free exploration within an inquiry framework. The latter are more likely to see their role as one of "sage on the stage" whereby they introduce complex learning to the student in a series of small, progressive, mediated steps.

In reality, teachers' complex tasks in classrooms mean they end up playing both these roles and several others. In terms of "assessment for learning" some teachers seek social, connected and distributed learning outcomes; others seek clear, objective learning outcomes. Some envisage content as discipline-related information, and assessment as a tracking of knowledge acquisition by the student; others see content as process, and assessment as student reflection.

In our experience, an understanding of SOLO Taxonomy helps teachers and students comprehend learning regardless of their pedagogical approach. This section offers a first step in building this understanding with an overview of SOLO Taxonomy and of key ways in which it is useful in schools.

## What is SOLO Taxonomy?

*It helps us to learn. It helps you to think and do a few things that you want to do. Because it helps you connect ideas and learn and think in your head.*

Year 1 student describes learning with SOLO Taxonomy (Hook, in press)

SOLO Taxonomy provides a simple and robust way of describing how learning outcomes grow in complexity from surface to deep to conceptual understanding (Biggs and Collis 1982). It describes five levels of understanding for students who are encountering new learning (Table 1). The distinction between each level is clearly categorised; teachers and students tend to agree on the SOLO level of a learning outcome.

**Table I: Levels of understanding in SOLO Taxonomy**

   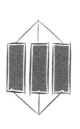 

| Prestructural | Unistructural | Multistructural | Relational | Extended abstract |
|---|---|---|---|---|
| Learning outcomes show unconnected information, with no organisation. | Learning outcomes show simple connections but importance of different parts is not noted. | Learning outcomes show connections are made, but significance of parts to overall meaning is missing. | Learning outcomes show full connections are made, and synthesis of parts to the overall meaning. | Learning outcomes go beyond subject and links are made to other concepts – generalisations. |

At the **prestructural level** of understanding (**Whakarangaranga**), the student attacks the task inappropriately; they may collect information but it has no organisation or connection and may be irrelevant. It may be that they have missed the point or need help to start. For example:

> *"I am not sure what a habitat is. I think it might be a skateboard company."*
> *"I need help to define habitat."*

The next two levels, unistructural and multistructural, are associated with bringing in information. At the **unistructural level** (**Rangaranga Takitahi**), the student picks up one aspect of the task and their understanding is disconnected and limited. For example:

> *"A habitat is a place."*
> *"My definition statement has one relevant idea about habitat."*

The jump to the multistructural level is quantitative. At the **multistructural level** (**Rangaranga Maha**), the student knows several aspects of the task but misses their relationships to each other and the whole. For example:

> As for unistructural plus: *"Plants and animals live in habitats. Different habitats are characterised by different living things."*
> *"My definition statement has several relevant ideas about habitat."*

The progression to relational and extended abstract outcomes is qualitative. At the **relational level** (**Whanaungatanga**), the student links and integrates the aspects, which contribute to a coherent understanding of the whole. For example:

> As for multistructural plus: *"This is because the different environmental factors in a habitat affect an organism's chances of survival and reproduction. For example, the environmental factors in a lake habitat are suited to the survival and reproduction of ducks, swans, water beetles, leeches and floating duckweed."*
> *"My definition statement has several relevant ideas about habitat, and links these in some way."*

At the **extended abstract level** (**Waitara Whānui**), the student rethinks their new understanding at the relational level, looks at it in a new way, and uses it as the basis for prediction, generalisation, reflection or creation of new understanding. For example:

> As for relational plus: *"I think we should care more about habitats, because changes affect the survival and reproduction of the organisms that live there."*
> *"My definition statement has several relevant ideas about habitat, links these and looks at these linked ideas in a new way."*

Template I sets out each level with its symbol and may be enlarged as a poster for the classroom. Thereafter Templates 2 and 3 (presented in landscape, although portrait would work equally well) offer the basis for a self assessment rubric for functioning and declarative knowledge respectively.

# Structure of Observed Learning Outcomes:

# SOLO Taxonomy

| Prestructural | Unistructural | Multistructural | Relational | Extended abstract |

Source: Developed from Biggs and Collis (1982)

# Template 2: Self assessment rubric (co-constructed) for SOLO functioning knowledge

| Prestructural | Unistructural | Multistructural | Relational | Extended abstract | |
|---|---|---|---|---|---|
| Learning outcomes show unconnected information, with no organisation. Example: "I need help or direction." | Learning outcomes show simple connections but importance of different parts is not noted. Examples: "I will have a tilt at it." "I can do it if directed." | Learning outcomes show connections are made, but significance of parts to overall meaning is missing. Example: "I will use trial and error to find a solution." | Learning outcomes show full connections are made, and synthesis of parts to the overall meaning. Example: "I plan to do X because it will ... I know what to do and why." | Learning outcomes go beyond subject and links are made to other concepts – generalisations. Examples: "I sense what to do to find the best solution." "I seek feedback and adjust my actions in response." | |

# Template 3: Self assessment rubric (co-constructed) for SOLO declarative knowledge

| | | | |
|---|---|---|---|
| **Extended abstract** | Learning outcomes go beyond subject and links are made to other concepts – generalisations. | | |
| **Relational** | Learning outcomes show full connections are made, and synthesis of parts to the overall meaning. | | |
| **Multistructural** | Learning outcomes show connections are made, but significance of parts to overall meaning is missing. | | |
| **Unistructural** | Learning outcomes show simple connections but importance of different parts is not noted. | | |
| **Prestructural** | Learning outcomes show unconnected information, with no organisation. | | |

# Why is SOLO Taxonomy useful?

*With teachers using the SOLO framework we have been given the tools to achieve and understand what is going on – it is not all in the teachers' hands which allows us to take responsibility for our own learning which in turn also gives us a sort of freedom which is useful and a feeling of control over our own learning.*

Year 12 student describes learning with SOLO Taxonomy (Hook, in press)

SOLO is useful because it makes learning outcomes visible to teachers and to students and their parents. By offering a clear, simple, and robust way of identifying the level of cognitive complexity of a learning intention and outcome (Biggs 1999, p 37), it improves the quality and effectiveness of feedback conversations in teaching and learning (Hook 2006, p 100).

Feedback prompts students (and teachers) to engage with the content, processes and/or self regulation needed to meet an identified learning outcome (Hattie 2011, p 174). Many teachers find it an ongoing challenge to make feedback more effective by improving its clarity, purpose, logic, meaning and/or proximity to existing understanding. However, when teachers and students use SOLO for evaluating their learning outcomes (and for identifying where best to target new learning experiences), they have a mental model of differentiated learning outcomes to reference feedback. They appear better able to engage in effective feedback when they understand learning outcomes through SOLO; students as young as five years old can self assess and peer assess their learning outcomes, offering SOLO-coded:

- "feedback" on how well they are going
- "feed up" on where they are going
- "feed forward" on the next steps in learning.

Furthermore the discriminators between levels in SOLO are stable, consistent and obvious, enabling students and teachers to achieve a clarity and consistency of understanding that helps throughout the teaching and learning process.

Students can more easily monitor, regulate and reflect on their own task understanding, and give effective feedback to teachers and peers on what happens next. For example, students use SOLO to:

- help clarify the purpose of learning intentions
- explain the selection of effective strategies
- self assess learning outcomes with SOLO-coded success criteria (in text-based or visual rubrics)
- create their "where to next" steps in learning logs.

For example, one pair wrote:

*We think our work is extended abstract because it includes similarities and differences, it also has target vocabulary such as overall and we think. Next time we will try to include a statement about what could happen in the future.*

Teachers use SOLO Taxonomy in planning to identify, describe, align and create learning intentions, learning experiences, success criteria and "assessment for learning" at different levels of cognitive complexity to meet the expectations of inclusion, coherence and high expectations (New Zealand Curriculum Principles) in the curriculum achievement objectives and achievement standards. Much like their students, teachers find that SOLO clarifies their inquiry into pedagogical practice, assisting them to monitor, regulate and reflect on the effectiveness of their teaching and to produce more effective feedback in prompting next steps for learning.

# 2. How can schools, teachers and students use SOLO Taxonomy?

*I think that SOLO helps us by letting you do things for yourself not someone doing it for you.*

Year 6 student describes learning with SOLO Taxonomy (Hook, in press)

School communities can enhance effective feedback conversations by using SOLO Taxonomy to create a common understanding of the learning outcomes. These feedback conversations address both **declarative knowledge** (knowing about things) and **functioning knowledge** (performance based on knowing about things).

To enable effective feedback conversations, schools adopt SOLO Taxonomy as a model of learning outcomes across all learning areas. This approach involves:

- displaying symbols representing SOLO levels, signing SOLO levels and talking about different SOLO learning outcomes across the school

- introducing a common language of learning verbs aligned to SOLO outcomes

- using these SOLO verbs in the process of constructive alignment to unpack achievement objectives and achievement standards and to develop learning intentions for learning experiences and assessment for learning

- designing appropriate "assessment for learning" tasks to develop understanding of a concept, learning intention, achievement objective or achievement standard

- using student learning logs as a way of recording student feedback (how well I am going) and feed up (where to next) reflections as part of their self assessment on the initial feed up (where am I going) task

- referencing effective strategies for SOLO learning verbs (HOT SOLO maps) and success criteria in self assessment rubrics (HOT SOLO map rubrics) for achieving identified learning outcomes across all learning areas.

This section offers suggestions and materials for implementing the first five actions above. Using effective strategies and success criteria is the central focus of Section 3.

## SOLO on display – talking about and seeing SOLO levels in all learning areas

When implementing SOLO as a model of learning outcomes, schools make SOLO posters visible across the campus, displaying them on all school walls – including in classrooms, library, staffroom and resource rooms.

SOLO symbols are used with students to code all learning intentions in "We are learning to" (WALT) and "I am learning to" (IALT) statements in class (Figure 1).

SOLO levels and hand signals are also used in oral and written feedback between students and between students and teachers. Template 4 is a poster of hand signals for display (as one possible set of signals – schools do vary in their choice of hand signals).

## Figure 1: SOLO-coded WALT

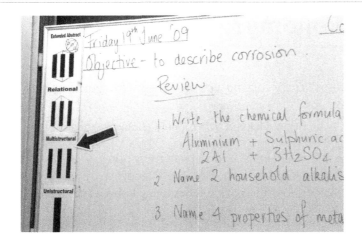

## Template 4: SOLO hand signals

Prestructural     Unistructural     Multistructural

Relational     Extended abstract

# SOLO learning verbs – a common language of learning

*I use the SOLO Taxonomy in all my subjects, it helps me plan out what I am writing, what I am doing, how to work things out. If I want to get this far I have to chuck in some relational aspects of it … and once you have written your essay, your paragraph you can reflect back on it or think about what you have done, evaluate how you have done your work and kind of reapply it, try a bit harder, change it to show extended abstract thinking.*

Year 11 students describe learning with SOLO Taxonomy (Hook, in press)

Associating the levels in SOLO with "declarative knowledge verbs" in the process of "constructive alignment" (Biggs and Tang 2007, p 79) is fundamental to building clarity, competence and confidence into the process of writing learning intentions. In New Zealand the list of SOLO-coded learning verbs for declarative and functioning knowledge (Table 2) has been selected from common task descriptors in the National Certificate of Educational Achievement (NCEA) (Hook, in press).

It is worth noting that these verb alignments are never absolute. Levelling verbs against SOLO outcomes can be ambiguous and needs to be "done in context" (Biggs and Tang 2007). In addition, because students at the prestructural level need teacher help to achieve learning outcomes and do not complete tasks in an appropriate or meaningful way, learning verbs are not applicable at this level.

## Table 2: SOLO declarative and functioning learning verbs

| SOLO level | Verbs |
|---|---|
| Unistructural | define, identify, name, draw, find, label, match, follow a simple procedure |
| Multistructural | describe, list, outline, follow an algorithm, combine |
| Relational | sequence, classify, compare and contrast, explain causes, explain effects, analyse (part–whole), form an analogy, organise, distinguish, interview, question, relate, apply |
| Extended abstract | generalise, predict, evaluate, reflect, hypothesise, theorise, create, prove, plan, justify, argue, compose, prioritise, design, construct, perform |

The SOLO theory about teaching and learning is based on research into student learning. As such it has many advantages over Bloom's cognitive taxonomy (Bloom 1965), which is a theory about knowledge based on the judgements of educational administrators (see Hattie and Brown 2004; Biggs and Tang 2007, p 80). Notably SOLO provides teachers with a more straightforward way of using learning verbs to write differentiated learning intentions, for the following reasons:

- Verb lists in Bloom are not reliable – *identify*, for example, is found in both Knowledge and Comprehension and *compare and contrast* in Evaluation and Analysis.

- A teacher attempting to write a learning intention at the Understanding level of Bloom's revised taxonomy has a broad array of verbs to choose from, including *classify, compare, exemplify, conclude, demonstrate, discuss, explain, identify, illustrate, interpret, paraphrase, predict* and *report* (Anderson and Krathwohl 2001). However, SOLO helps to target the learning intention more precisely, by differentiating such verbs into three levels of learning outcome.

- SOLO's differentiation of levels also enables teachers and students to identify and categorise learning outcomes easily and to design the follow-up learning experience at a level to challenge yet not overwhelm.

- With SOLO, in contrast to Bloom's taxonomy, a learning task can sit at one level of cognitive complexity while the learning outcomes can be assessed across five different levels of complexity.

# Constructive alignment

Constructive alignment involves using the SOLO verbs to unpack an achievement objective or achievement standard. It helps teachers (and students) understand how to scaffold learning intentions for deep conceptual understanding (Biggs and Tang 2007, p 50). The process outcomes provide clear guidelines on how to move students from surface to deep to conceptual understanding. In addition, when SOLO learning verbs are shared with students they enhance feed up between students and teachers – that is, conversations on "How well am I doing?" and "Why am I doing it?"

In constructive alignment, teachers use SOLO declarative and functioning knowledge verbs (Table 2 on the previous page) to write learning intentions. The SOLO verbs help them to unpack New Zealand Curriculum achievement objectives and achievement standards against SOLO levels. Table 3 gives an example of this process, drawing on the science curriculum.

**Table 3: Constructive alignment – Achievement Standard Science 1.1: Demonstrate understanding of aspects of mechanics**

| Ask: What can be ...? | Achievement Standard Science 1.1: Demonstrate understanding of aspects of mechanics |
|---|---|
| *defined* | Distance; speed; velocity; distance/speed–time graphs; acceleration; deceleration; mass; weight; balanced forces; unbalanced forces; stationary; constant speed; force; pressure; work; power; gravitational potential energy; kinetic energy; conservation of energy |
| *described* | Distance/speed–time graphs of journeys etc; the relationship $v = d/t$; the relationship $a = v/t$; forces on a stationary object; forces on a moving object, at constant speed and accelerating; the relationship $F = ma$; pressure on everyday objects; the relationship $P = F/A$; energy changes of freefalling objects; energy changes of everyday experiences; the relationship $E_p = mgh$; the relationship $E_k = \frac{1}{2}mv^2$; the relationship $W = Fd$; the relationship $P = W/t$ |
| *sequenced* | The distance and speed changes of a journey; the energy changes of an everyday object |
| *classified* | The types of forces; the types of energy |
| *compared* | Distance–time graphs to speed–time graphs; acceleration to deceleration; velocity to speed; mass to weight; balanced forces to unbalanced forces |
| *explained* | Of an object moving at constant speed; of an object accelerating; of pressure; of energy changes |
| *analysed* | Distance–time graphs; speed–time graphs |
| *predicted* | The velocity of an object changes; the forces acting on an object changes; the area of an object, or its force, changes |
| *generalised* | About the relationship $F = ma$; about the relationship $P = F/A$; about the conservation of mechanical energy |

*Source: Adapted from Georgina Barrett, Head of Department, Science, Lincoln High School*

The outcomes of the constructive alignment process are shown in Tables 4 and 5 where SOLO verbs are selected at the appropriate level of understanding for the achievement objective or standard. The content and contexts chosen are appropriate to the achievement objective/standard and/or to local communities of practice. Template 5 offers a format for achieving constructive alignment in planning for an achievement or objective or standard.

**Table 4: Using SOLO verbs to align learning intentions with an achievement objective**

| New Zealand Curriculum Achievement objective | SOLO level | Learning intentions |
|---|---|---|
| *Science* <br><br> *Material World* <br><br> *Level One* <br><br> *Properties and changes of matter* <br><br> Observe, describe and compare physical and chemical properties of common materials and changes that occur when materials are mixed, heated or cooled. | Unistructural | *Define* properties. <br> *Define* physical properties. <br> *Define* chemical properties. <br> *Define* materials. <br> *Define* common material. <br> *Define* mixture/heating/cooling. <br> *Observe* mixing/heating/cooling of common materials. |
| | Multistructural | *Describe* common materials. <br> *Describe* mixing/heating/cooling of common materials. <br> *Describe* physical properties of common materials. <br> *Describe* chemical properties of common materials. |
| | Relational | *Sequence* the changes when common materials are mixed (heated or cooled). <br> *Classify* the properties of common materials. <br> *Compare and contrast* physical and chemical properties of common materials. <br> *Compare and contrast* the changes that occur when common materials are mixed (heated or cooled). <br> *Explain* the causes of the changes that occur when common materials are mixed (heated or cooled). |
| | Extended abstract | *Predict* what might happen when common materials are mixed (heated or cooled). <br> *Generalise* about the changes that occur when common materials are mixed (heated or cooled). <br> *Create* an action to change a common material by mixing (cooling or heating). |

Source of curriculum information: Adapted from Ministry of Education. (2007). *The New Zealand Curriculum for English-medium Teaching and Learning in Years 1–13.* Wellington: Learning Media.

## Table 5: Using SOLO verbs to align learning intentions with an achievement standard

| Student learning outcome | SOLO level | Learning intention |
|---|---|---|
| Demonstrate understanding of aspects of mechanics, specifically:<br><br>distance, speed, interpretation of distance– and speed–time graphs, average acceleration and deceleration in the context of everyday experiences such as journeys, sport, getting going, etc the relationships:<br><br>$v = \dfrac{\Delta v}{\Delta t}$ and a $= \dfrac{\Delta d}{\Delta t}$. | Unistructural | *Define* terms associated with motion – distance, speed, velocity, distance–time graphs, speed–time graphs, acceleration, deceleration. |
| | Multistructural | *Describe* the distance, speed, velocity changes of a journey.<br><br>*Describe* distance–time and speed–time graphs.<br><br>*Describe* the relationships:<br><br>$v = \dfrac{\Delta v}{\Delta t}$ and a $= \dfrac{\Delta d}{\Delta t}$. |
| | Relational | *Sequence* the distance and speed changes of a journey.<br><br>*Compare and contrast* velocity with speed.<br><br>*Compare and contrast* distance–time graphs with speed–time graphs.<br><br>*Compare and contrast* acceleration with deceleration.<br><br>*Analyse* distance– and speed–time graphs. |
| | Extended abstract | *Predict* what might happen to distance– and speed–time graphs when velocity changes. |

Sources:

Curriculum information: Ministry of Education. (2007). *The New Zealand Curriculum for English-medium Teaching and Learning in Years 1–13.* Wellington: Learning Media.

SOLO alignment: Georgina Barrett, Head of Department, Science, Lincoln High School

Template 5: SOLO constructive alignment

| Achievement objective (AO) or achievement standard (AS): [Insert here] | | |
|---|---|---|
| **Multistructural level** | **Relational level** | **Extended abstract level** |
| Use SOLO learning verbs to clarify the AO or AS learning objective by asking the following: | | |
| What can be defined?<br>What can be described?<br>What can be observed? | What can be sequenced?<br>What can be classified?<br>What can be compared and contrasted?<br>What can be explained? (cause and effect)<br>What can be analysed? (part–whole)<br>What can be made into an analogy? | What can be generalised?<br>What can be predicted?<br>What can be evaluated?<br>What can be created?<br>What can be reflected on? |
| **Review** the potential learning intentions (LIs) above against SMART criteria (specific, measurable, attainable, relevant, time-bound).<br><br>**Write learning intentions** necessary for understanding the AO or AS at three SOLO levels. | | |
| **Multistructural LIs** | **Relational LIs** | **Extended abstract LIs** |
| Students should be able to:<br><br>LI: [verb] [content] [context]<br><br>LI: [verb] [content] [context]<br><br>LI: [verb] [content] [context] | Students should be able to:<br><br>LI: [verb] [content] [context]<br><br>LI: [verb] [content] [context]<br><br>LI: [verb] [content] [context] | Students should be able to:<br><br>LI: [verb] [content] [context]<br><br>LI: [verb] [content] [context]<br><br>LI: [verb] [content] [context] |

## Designing three-level "assessment for learning" tasks

Identifying appropriate "assessment for learning" tasks to develop understanding of a concept, learning intention, achievement objective or achievement standard is easier if the tasks are selected across the multistructural, relational and extended abstract levels of SOLO. If three tasks are selected, one from each level, students (and their teachers) can more reliably assess the evidence for the cognitive complexity of their understanding.

The structure of the task is constructed as: **[SOLO learning verb] [content] [context]**. Examples of the verbs used are:

- at the multistructural level, declarative learning verbs like *define* and *describe*
- at the relational level, learning verbs like *sequence, classify, compare and contrast* and *analyse*
- at the extended abstract level, declarative and functioning learning verbs like *generalise, evaluate, predict, reflect, create*.

Table 6 on the next page sets out an example of three-level assessment tasks used to collect evidence for understanding of te ao Māori macroconcepts. Then Template 6 offers one format for implementing three-level assessment tasks in any subject.

**Table 6: SOLO three-level "assessment for learning" tasks for te ao Māori macroconcepts**

| SOLO level | Tūrangawaewae – a place to stand | Kaitiakitanga – guardianship | Tino rangatiratanga – self-management, determination | Whanaungatanga – relationships, connectedness | Whakataukī – stories, proverbs and communication |
|---|---|---|---|---|---|
| Multistructural | Describe tūrangawaewae for an individual or group. | Define kaitiakitanga. | Define tino rangatiratanga. | Describe whanaungatanga. | Retell a whakataukī. |
| Relational | Explain how a space/place became a tūrangawaewae for an individual or group. | Explain the effect of kaitiakitanga on a local environment. | Compare and contrast the role of tino rangatiratanga in the past with its role in the present. | Analyse the important parts of whanaungatanga. | Explain the message communicated in a whakataukī. |
| Extended abstract | Reflect on the importance of tūrangawaewae to an individual or group. | Predict what might happen in the future if we do not live in a way that values kaitiakitanga. | Evaluate the significance of tino rangatiratanga to New Zealanders today. | Make a generalisation about whanaungatanga. | Create a whakataukī to communicate a message. |

## Template 6: HOT learning log – three-level assessment task

| Learning area: | | Level: |
|---|---|---|

| Achievement objective/achievement standard: |
|---|
|  |

| Learning intention 1: Multistructural |
|---|
| [Multistructural learning verb eg, *define, describe*] [content] [context] |

| Success criteria | | |
|---|---|---|
| Prestructural | | self/peer |
| Unistructural | | self/peer |
| Multistructural | | self/peer |
| Relational | | self/peer |
| Extended abstract | | self/peer |

| Learning intention 2: Relational |
|---|
| [Relational learning verb eg, *sequence, classify, compare and contrast, explain causes, explain effects, analyse (part–whole), form an analogy, form a question*] [content] [context] |

| Success criteria | | |
|---|---|---|
| Prestructural | | self/peer |
| Unistructural | | self/peer |
| Multistructural | | self/peer |
| Relational | | self/peer |
| Extended abstract | | self/peer |

| Learning intention 3: Extended abstract |
|---|
| [Extended abstract learning verb eg, *generalise, predict, evaluate, create*] [content] [context] |

| Success criteria | | |
|---|---|---|
| Prestructural | | self/peer |
| Unistructural | | self/peer |
| Multistructural | | self/peer |
| Relational | | self/peer |
| Extended abstract | | self/peer |

# Student learning logs

*Tino pai rawa atu te Akoranga nei natemea, ka taea e au ki te ako i te kaupapa, ki te whakamārama i te kaupapa me te mōhio kei hea te taumata māku. Ka mōhio au mehemea kei te taumata "whakarangaranga" ka piki ake taku mātauranga ki te tae atu ki te "rangaranga takitahi". Kei te taumata "rangaranga" maha au ētahi wā kei "whanaungatanga" heoi anō ko te wawata kia tae atu ki "waitara whānui" natemea ko tērā te taumata teitei mōku. He rawe te kawe tahi i te ako o ngā kaupapa i te taha o te Kaiako, natemea ka tū rangatira au.*

Tauira tau whā

*Translation: I enjoy using SOLO rubrics because I can self assess and peer assess, and everyone knows where they are in their learning. I know that if I start at prestructural I need a lot more help from the teacher, and my main goal would be unistructural learning. I am not at prestructural or unistructural, but at multistructural and sometimes relational, and my main goal is to be extended abstract. I like how we share the learning in the class; it makes me feel important.*

Year 4 student describes learning with SOLO Taxonomy (Hook, in press)

Students can use SOLO rubrics based on three-level tasks to self assess and their feedback (how well I am going) and feed up (where to next) reflections, which they record in student learning logs. The following examples illustrate some of the forms such reflections may take.

A student learning log entry for the concept of kaitiakitanga reads:

*My learning outcome for understanding "kaitiakitanga" is relational because I can explain the effect of kaitiakitanga on my local environment. My next step is to explore what might happen in the future if we do not live in a way that values kaitiakitanga.*

In a learning log statement for *define* a six-year-old reflects:

*My learning outcome is relational because I have used two linking words. My next step is to use more linking words.*

In a learning log statement for *discuss* a 17-year-old reflects:

*My learning outcome is multistructural because I didn't explain it enough. Next time I will add my becauses in to get to the next level.*

Figure 2 shows a learning log recording SOLO-coded student learning outcomes for a Year 2–3 class. Template 7 is a poster that puts the role of the learning log in context as the concluding part of the SOLO process of achieving learning outcomes.

## Figure 2: Student learning log with SOLO-coded learning outcomes

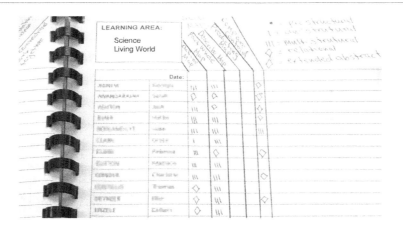

## Template 7: Overview of the key ingredients in achieving a learning outcome

Learning Intention, Effective Strategy, Success Criteria, Learning Log

1. Identify the learning intention.

    [verb] [content] [context]

2. Identify an effective strategy to support the learning intention.

    HOT SOLO maps:

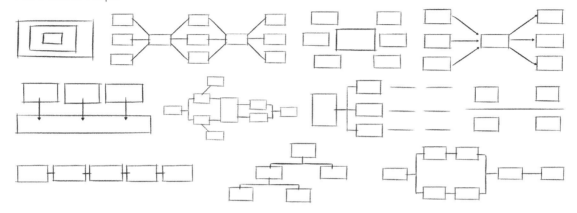

3. Identify success criteria for the effective strategy in order to assess learning outcomes.

    HOT SOLO self assessment rubrics:

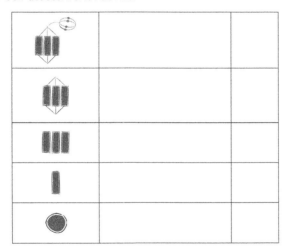

4. Create a SOLO learning log for self and/or peer assessment

Effective strategy:

*SOLO learning log*

My [statement] is at a [insert SOLO level] outcome because …

My next step is to …

# 3. Effective strategies and success criteria

This section shows how teachers and students can employ effective strategies to achieve learning intentions and construct success criteria for assessment by using a combination of: HOT SOLO maps; target vocabulary; and self assessment rubrics.

It provides guidance on using different types of HOT SOLO maps and their accompanying rubrics, as well as templates for each one that can be adopted and/or adapted and put to use in the classroom.

## What are HOT SOLO maps?

HOT SOLO maps clarify the nature of the learning task – the maps act as effective strategies for each declarative SOLO verb. There are HOT SOLO maps for:

- bringing in ideas – unistructural and multistructural learning outcomes (*define, describe*)
- connecting ideas – relational learning outcomes (*sequence, classify, compare and contrast, explain causes and effects, analyse, form an analogy*)
- looking at connected ideas in a new way (*generalise, reflect, predict, justify, evaluate*).

## How do HOT SOLO maps work together with target vocabulary and self assessment rubrics?

HOT SOLO maps, target vocabulary and self assessment rubrics have been designed to work together as effective strategies and success criteria to help students understand what they are doing, how it is going and what they should do next.

Target vocabulary accompanies each HOT SOLO map (Figure 3) to support student literacy outcomes. By way of introduction to the specific HOT SOLO maps, a selection of templates follows:

- Template 8 provides a broader framework for effective strategies, encompassing learning intentions, self assessment rubrics, and student feedback (how well I am going) and feed up (where to next).
- Template 9 links each HOT SOLO map to its target vocabulary.
- Template 10 shows how the various HOT SOLO maps are paired with learning verbs at the different SOLO levels. Students can use this overview to monitor their introduction and use of HOT SOLO maps.
- Template 11 links the learning verb for each HOT SOLO map to a range of literacy outcomes.

### Figure 3: Target vocabulary for sequencing

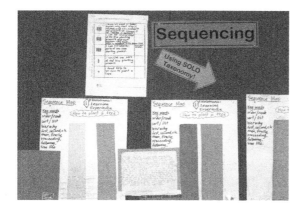

# Template 8: Putting the effective strategy (HOT SOLO map) within a broader framework

## Learning intention

I am learning to [SOLO verb] [content] [context]

For example: *I am learning to describe the habitat of the tuna (eel) in the Ngongotaha Stream.*

## Effective strategy

Choose the appropriate HOT SOLO map aligned to the learning verb.

For example: *Student uses a HOT SOLO Describe map and success criteria in the self assessment rubric to plan their description.*

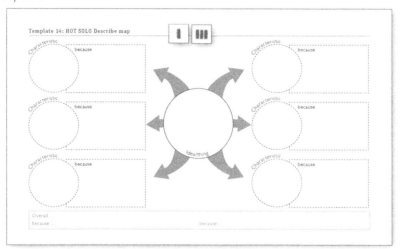

## Target vocabulary

Insert target and technical vocabulary.

For example: *and, in addition, as well as, also, too, for example, another, because, overall*

## Success criteria

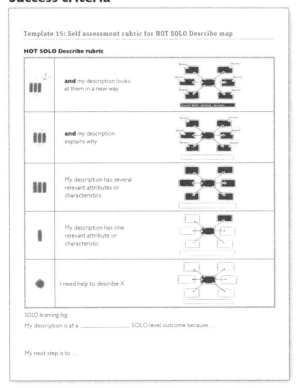

## Learning outcome

For example: Student describes in writing or orally, or creates an annotated diagram of, the habitat of the tuna in the Ngongotaha Stream.

### Feedback (How well am I going?)

My learning outcome is [insert SOLO level] because …

### Feed up (Where to next?)

My next step is to …

## Template 9: Target vocabulary for HOT SOLO maps

| Outcomes | Vocabulary | |
|---|---|---|
| *Multistructural level* | | |
| HOT SOLO Define map and self assessment rubric<br><br>HOT SOLO Describe map and self assessment rubric | and<br>in addition<br>as well as<br>also<br>too<br>moreover<br>apart from | besides<br>furthermore<br>what is more<br>not only … but also<br>another point is that<br>for example<br>another |
| *Relational level* | | |
| HOT SOLO Sequence map and self assessment rubric | after<br>after that<br>afterwards<br>as soon as<br>at first<br>at the beginning<br>at last<br>at the end<br>before<br>during<br>eventually<br>finally<br>first (of all)<br>first, second, finally<br>hardly … when<br>immediately<br>in the beginning | in the end<br>lastly<br>next<br>no sooner … than<br>on<br>once<br>prior to<br>soon<br>suddenly<br>the first point is<br>the following<br>the former, … the latter<br>then<br>to begin with<br>until when<br>while |
| HOT SOLO Cause and Effect map and self assessment rubric | **Cause**<br>as<br>because<br>because of<br>due to<br>due to the fact that<br>owing to<br>owing to the fact that<br>since<br>so | **Consequence/effect**<br>accordingly<br>as a result<br>consequently<br>due to this<br>for this reason<br>hence<br>in order that<br>in that case<br>not enough … for/to<br>on account of this<br>so<br>so … that<br>so as to<br>such … that<br>that being so<br>therefore<br>this is why<br>this means that<br>thus<br>to<br>too … for/to |

| Outcomes | Vocabulary | |
|---|---|---|
| HOT SOLO Compare and Contrast map and self assessment rubric | **Comparison**<br>a parallel argument<br>after all<br>also<br>as<br>at the same time<br>by and large<br>in a similar manner<br>in comparison<br>in the same manner<br>in the same way<br>like<br>likewise<br>meanwhile<br>similarly<br>simultaneously | **Contrast**<br>although<br>although this is<br>and yet<br>but<br>but although<br>conversely<br>despite<br>despite the fact that<br>even so<br>even though<br>for all that<br>however<br>in contrast<br>in spite of<br>in spite of the fact that<br>in theory … in practice …<br>neither … nor<br>nevertheless<br>nonetheless<br>notwithstanding<br>on the contrary<br>on the one hand<br>on the other hand<br>otherwise<br>still<br>true<br>unlike<br>whereas<br>while this is true<br>yet |
| *Extended abstract level* | | |
| HOT SOLO Generalise map and self assessment rubric | **Claim**<br>all in all<br>apparently<br>generally<br>I believe (that)<br>I think (that)<br>I would say that<br>in a nutshell<br>in brief<br>in conclusion<br>in my opinion<br>in short<br>in summary<br>in the main<br>on the whole<br>overall<br>personally<br>to conclude<br>to sum up<br>to summarise | **Giving reasons and grounds**<br>anecdotal<br>because … because<br>common knowledge<br>considered plausible<br>expert opinion<br>for example/eg<br>for instance<br>such as<br>for one thing<br>ie/that is<br>personal experience<br>this includes |

| Outcomes | Vocabulary | |
|---|---|---|
| HOT SOLO Evaluate map and self assessment rubric | **Claim**<br>the best solution is | **Reasons, helping premise and grounds**<br>anecdotal<br>because … because<br>common knowledge<br>considered plausible<br>expert opinion<br>personal experience |
| HOT SOLO Predict map and self assessment rubric | **Prediction**<br>I foresee a time when …<br>in the future | **Reasons and grounds anecdotal**<br>because … because<br>common knowledge<br>considered plausible<br>expert opinion<br>personal experience |

## Template 10: Overview of HOT SOLO maps paired with their learning verbs

| Prestructural | Unistructural | Multistructural | Relational | Extended abstract |
|---|---|---|---|---|
| | Define | Describe | Sequence | Generalise |
| | | | Classify | Predict |
| | | | Compare and contrast | Evaluate |
| | | | Cause and effect | |
| | | | Analyse | |
| | | | Analogy | |

# Template 11: Learning verbs and literacy outcomes

| SOLO level | Verb | Outcomes | | | | |
|---|---|---|---|---|---|---|
| Unistructural/ multistructural | *define* | Biographies<br>Definitions<br>Discussions | Explanations<br>Fact and opinion<br>Information reports | Narratives<br>Non-chronological reports<br>Non-fiction | Note taking<br>Science experiments | |
| | *describe* | Autobiographies<br>Biographies | Newspaper reports<br>TV/video reporting | Descriptive writing (setting, events, character, feature, plot, theme) | Children's CV | |
| Relational | *make an analogy* | Alliteration<br>Creative writing | Expressive writing<br>Metaphor and similes | Narrative<br>Poetic writing | Sonnets | |
| | *explain cause and effect* | Analysis of information<br>Brochures<br>Business letters | Casual explanation<br>Data collection<br>Fact and opinion | Leaflets<br>Letters to editor<br>Note taking | Primary and secondary sources<br>Report writing<br>Researching | |
| | *classify* | Autobiographies<br>Biographies<br>Historical reporting | Information reports<br>Itinerary writing<br>Non-chronological reports | Non-fiction<br>Presentations<br>Travel writing | Family histories (oral or written) | |
| | *compare and contrast* | Comparative writing<br>Information reports | Newspaper reports<br>Non-chronological reports | Presentations | | |
| | *analyse (part–whole)* | Advertising<br>Analysis<br>Analysis of information<br>Book reviews<br>Business letters | Characterisations<br>Data collection<br>Fact and opinion<br>Letters to editor<br>Non-chronological reports | Non-fiction<br>Primary and secondary sources<br>Report writing<br>Researching | Scientific/technological outcomes<br>Static images | |
| Extended abstract | *evaluate* | Advertising<br>Analysis of information<br>Argument writing<br>Blogging<br>Business letters | Data collection<br>Debating<br>Essays<br>Evaluative writing<br>Fact and opinion | Judgements<br>Letters to editor<br>Personal judgements<br>Persuasive writing<br>Primary and secondary sources | Report writing<br>Researching<br>Validity and reliability of information/data | |
| | *generalise* | Analysis of information<br>Blogging<br>Business letters | Data collection<br>Fact and opinion<br>Generalisations | Letters to editor<br>Personal judgements<br>Primary and secondary sources | Report writing<br>Researching<br>Validity and reliability of information/data | |
| | *predict* | Analysis of information<br>Blogging<br>Business letters<br>Data collection | Fact and opinion<br>Hypotheses<br>Judgements<br>Letters to editor | Personal judgements<br>Predicting outcomes in fiction<br>Primary and secondary sources<br>Report writing | Researching<br>Validity and reliability of information/data | |

# What are the benefits of this approach?

A significant advantage of using SOLO Taxonomy in clarifying feedback is that the task and the task outcomes can be at different levels. For example, if the learning intention is at a relational level then the learning outcome can be achieved at unistructural, multistructural, relational or extended abstract level. Therefore teachers and students can:

* co-construct success criteria against SOLO learning outcomes
* build self and peer assessment SOLO rubrics for declarative and functioning knowledge outcomes.

Thus with the HOT SOLO Compare and Contrast map (Template 20, page 43), the task is at the SOLO relational level because the process of comparison requires students to link relevant ideas. However, each student's comparison statement formed from the map can be coded against SOLO. The process of comparison asks students to identify relevant similarities and differences between [X] and [Y] which they can do by:

* listing similarities and differences (multistructural learning outcome)
* listing and explaining, why they are similar and/or different (relational learning outcome)
* listing, explaining, generalising about or evaluating the extent of the similarity or difference (extended abstract learning outcome).

In this way the SOLO-differentiated outcomes for each learning verb act as explicit success criteria for students, providing feedback and feed forward on the learning intention and outcome.

Each HOT SOLO map is accompanied by a visual SOLO-coded self assessment rubric (although text-based rubrics are another option: see Figure 4), allowing students to reflect on the SOLO level of their learning outcome and "where to next". For example, a student learning log might read:

 *My learning outcome is at a relational level because I have linked ideas by explaining them. My next step is to look at the big picture and make a generalisation about these linked ideas.*

## Figure 4: Examples of HOT SOLO map use and student self assessment against SOLO rubrics

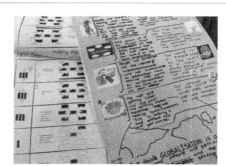

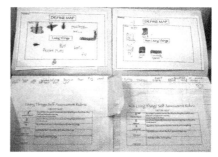

a. Visual rubric          b. Text-based rubric

Each HOT SOLO map and self assessment rubric can be used for formative and summative assessment – as pre and post knowledge tests for assessment purposes and as a series of snapshots of the learning process throughout a topic. Students will be able to see the progress that they have made and be able to reflect on how their learning outcomes change over time.

Because of the explicit nature of SOLO learning outcomes at all levels, students are soon able to select the appropriate HOT SOLO map for an identified learning intention and to construct their own success criteria against SOLO for both declarative and functioning knowledge outcomes. They can self regulate their learning by asking, answering and auctioning: *Where am I? How well am I doing? What do I do next?*

# Overview of HOT SOLO maps

The subsections that follow set out a variety of HOT SOLO maps and their accompanying self assessment rubrics for the different SOLO levels, with templates and more detailed instructions on how to use each one.

To construct a HOT SOLO map at any level, teachers and students may use text (Post-it notes), images, graphics, photographs, student drawings or physical objects to represent ideas. Each map also has a set of target vocabulary, which becomes the basis of a schoolwide common language, and a set of suggested literacy outcomes to support the curriculum (see Templates 9 and 11 above).

## Unistructural and multistructural HOT SOLO maps

**SOLO verbs:** *define, describe*

The HOT SOLO maps at the unistructural and multistructural levels are effective strategies for bringing in relevant ideas and information. These maps can be used to determine prior knowledge and for new learning.

Each map is accompanied by a self assessment rubric which provides success criteria for *define* and *describe* learning intentions.

## Relational HOT SOLO maps

**SOLO verbs:** *sequence, classify, compare and contrast, explain cause and effect, analyse (part–whole), form an analogy*

The HOT SOLO relational maps are effective strategies for connecting and relating relevant ideas and information. Students will be able to achieve deeper learning outcomes if they have first clarified terms using the unistructural and multistructural HOT SOLO Define and Describe maps.

Each map is accompanied by a self assessment rubric which provides success criteria for learning intentions targeting s*equencing, classifying, comparing, analysing, explaining cause or effect, forming analogies* or other relational activities.

## Extended abstract HOT SOLO maps

**SOLO verbs:** *generalise, predict, evaluate*

The HOT SOLO extended abstract maps are strategies that help students put their new learning into another context. This learning stage requires students to judge, evaluate, generalise, predict, theorise and create new ideas. If they have engaged with the HOT SOLO unistructural, multistructural and relational maps previously then they will be better prepared for using the HOT SOLO maps at the extended abstract level and achieve deeper learning outcomes. The HOT SOLO extended abstract maps also develop and support information literacy skills and critical thinking so students can research effectively and can evidence their findings.

Each HOT SOLO map is supported by a HOT SOLO rubric which sets out success criteria for learning intentions targeting *generalising, predicting* and *evaluating.*

The templates provided need not limit you as you can use Post-it notes to add extra features as required.

Initially teachers tend to use the HOT SOLO extended abstract maps as teaching tools. However, the maps are more successful once students are able to select and use the appropriate ones to drive their own learning at this level and co-construct their own self assessment rubrics.

# Unistructural and multistructural HOT SOLO maps

## HOT SOLO Define map and self assessment rubric

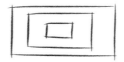

*Define – What is it?*

### What are these resources for?

You can use the HOT SOLO Define map and self assessment rubric to clarify the meaning of unknown ideas, vocabulary and terms.

### How do I use them?

1. Align the HOT SOLO Define map and self assessment rubric with the identified learning intention. For example, "We are learning to define [content] [context]."

2. Place the idea to be defined (main idea) in the centre of the map.

3. Add ideas related to the main idea in the "relevant" middle rectangle.

4. Clarify these ideas with students and move ideas that are not relevant to the "not relevant" outer rectangle.

   Note: If the students have not generated many ideas, give them the opportunity to improve their content understanding through books, ICTs, guest speakers etc. Then add their new ideas to the map and discuss their relevance with students.

5. Explain the identified ideas and make links between them.

6. Make a generalisation about the idea. For example, "Overall ... because ... because ..."

7. Share with students the success criteria for definition in the HOT SOLO Define rubric.

8. With reference to the success criteria, students make definition statements using the ideas and the target vocabulary from the completed HOT SOLO Define map. They may draw, write or say these statements. This process is iterative, meaning that students can repeat it whenever new learning occurs and thus can improve on the original definition statement.

9. Students self or peer assess their definition statements and seek teacher feedback on them.

10. Students assess their learning outcome for the identified learning intention against the SOLO levels, explain why they have chosen this level of learning outcome for their work (feedback) and suggest "where to next" steps (feed up).

11. Students record this work in their learning logs.

### Note

You can use the HOT SOLO Define map on a daily basis to develop new understandings of the topic you are teaching. After following the process above for one idea, place another idea in the centre box and move the words that are not relevant to that idea into the "not relevant" outer rectangle and repeat the process. In this way, as you add to the HOT SOLO Define map regularly, you start to build a contextual overview of the topic. By moving ideas and vocabulary in and out of the relevant box according to their relevance to the main idea, students also understand that defining involves sorting for relevance.

Template 12: HOT SOLO Define map

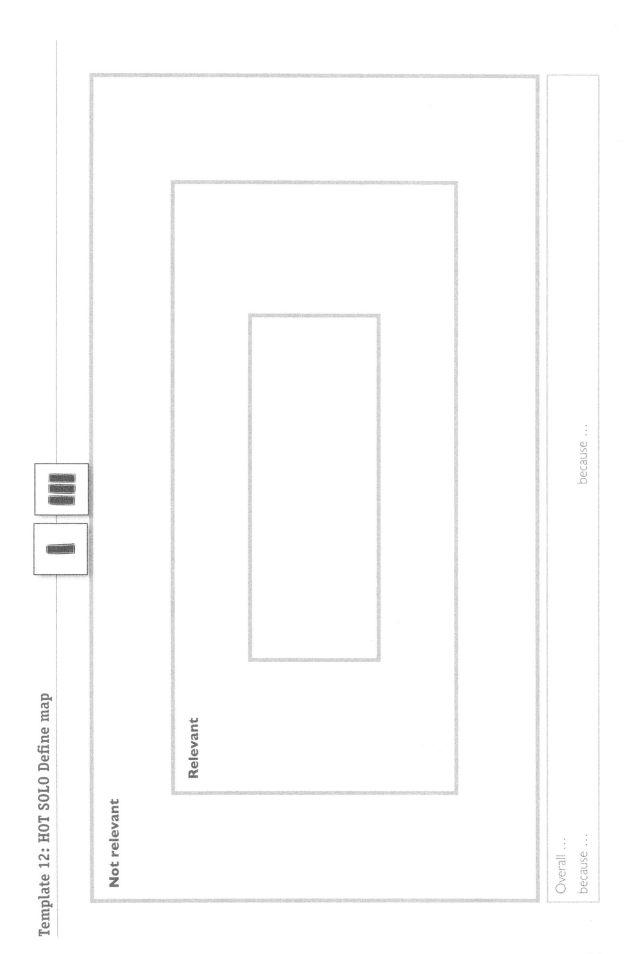

Not relevant

Relevant

Overall …
because …

because …

31

**HOT SOLO Define rubric**

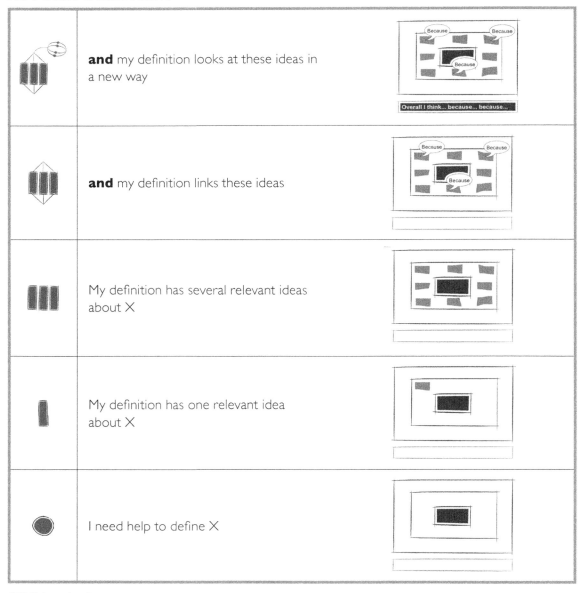

| | **and** my definition looks at these ideas in a new way | |
| | **and** my definition links these ideas | |
| | My definition has several relevant ideas about X | |
| | My definition has one relevant idea about X | |
| | I need help to define X | |

*SOLO learning log*

My definition statement is at a _____ SOLO level outcome because …

My next step is to …

## SOLO Describe map and self assessment rubric

*Describe – What is it like?*

**What are these resources for?**

You can use the HOT SOLO Describe map and self assessment rubric to identify the attributes or characteristics of an idea or object using adjectives and adjectival phrases.

**How do I use them?**

1. Align the HOT SOLO Describe map with the identified learning intention. For example, "We are learning to describe [content] [context]."

2. Place the idea or object to be described in the centre of the map.

3. Suggest possible attributes for description – such as the five senses, emotions, settings.

4. Record the relevant attributes in the "characteristic" circles that sit around the main idea.

5. Explain the identified characteristics and/or make links between them.

6. Make a generalisation about the description. For example, "Overall … because … because …"

7. Share with the students the success criteria for description in the HOT SOLO Describe rubric.

8. With reference to the success criteria, students describe an idea or object using the relevant characteristics and the target vocabulary from the completed HOT SOLO Describe map. They may write or say their description or present it in an annotated drawing. This process is iterative, meaning that students can repeat it whenever new learning occurs and thus can improve on the original description.

9. Students self or peer assess the descriptions and seek teacher feedback on them.

10. Students assess their learning outcome for the identified learning intention against the SOLO levels, explain why they have chosen this level of learning outcome for their work (feedback) and suggest "where to next" steps (feed up).

11. Students record this work in their learning logs.

# Template 14: HOT SOLO Describe map

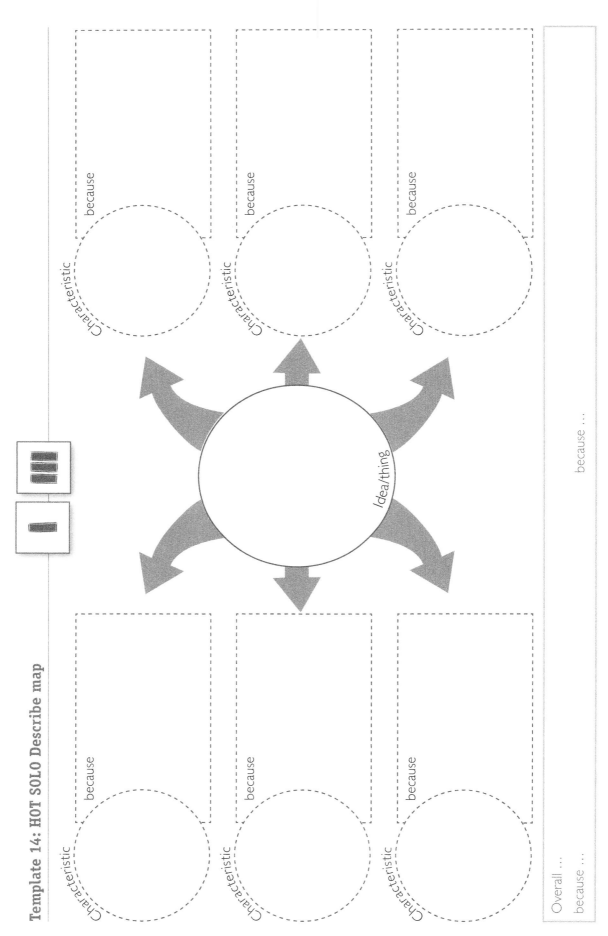

Characteristic ... because ...

Characteristic ... because ...

Characteristic ... because ...

Idea/thing

Characteristic ... because ...

Characteristic ... because ...

Characteristic ... because ...

Overall ...
because ...

because ...

34

**HOT SOLO Describe rubric**

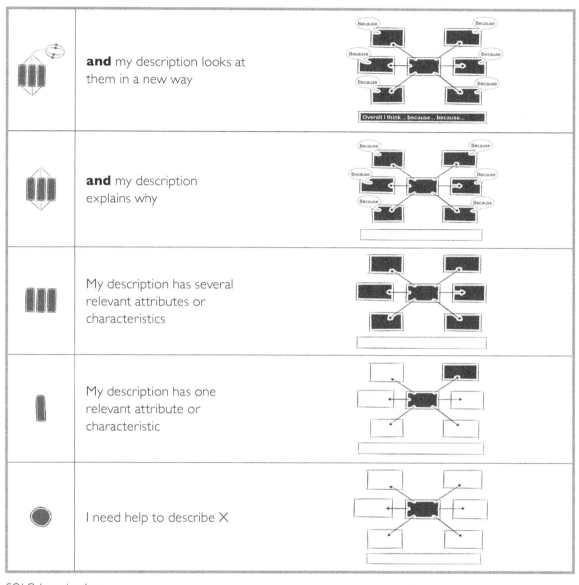

| | **and** my description looks at them in a new way | |
| | **and** my description explains why | |
| | My description has several relevant attributes or characteristics | |
| | My description has one relevant attribute or characteristic | |
| | I need help to describe X | |

*SOLO learning log*

My description is at a _____ SOLO level outcome because …

My next step is to …

## HOT SOLO Sequence map and self assessment rubric

*Sequence – What is the order?*

**What are these resources for?**

You can use the HOT SOLO Sequence map and self assessment rubric to clarify the sequence of ideas and events.

**How do I use them?**

1. Align the HOT SOLO Sequence map to the identified learning intention. For example, "We are learning to sequence [content] [context]."

2. Place the events in order. Use text, photographs or student drawings.

3. Put speech bubbles alongside each stage and use them to explain why each event is ordered like it is.

4. Make a generalisation about the sequence. For example, "Overall … because … because …"

5. Share the success criteria for sequencing in the HOT SOLO Sequence rubric.

6. With reference to the success criteria, students create statements to sequence an event using the target vocabulary from the completed HOT SOLO Sequence map. They can write or say these sequence statements or convey them through a series of annotated drawings. This process is iterative, meaning that students can repeat it whenever new learning occurs and thus can improve on the original sequence statements.

7. Students self or peer assess their sequence statements and seek teacher feedback on them.

8. Students assess their learning outcome for the identified learning intention against the SOLO levels, explain why they have chosen this level of learning outcome for their work (feedback) and suggest "where to next" steps (feed up).

9. Students record this work in their learning logs.

# Template 16: HOT SOLO Sequence map

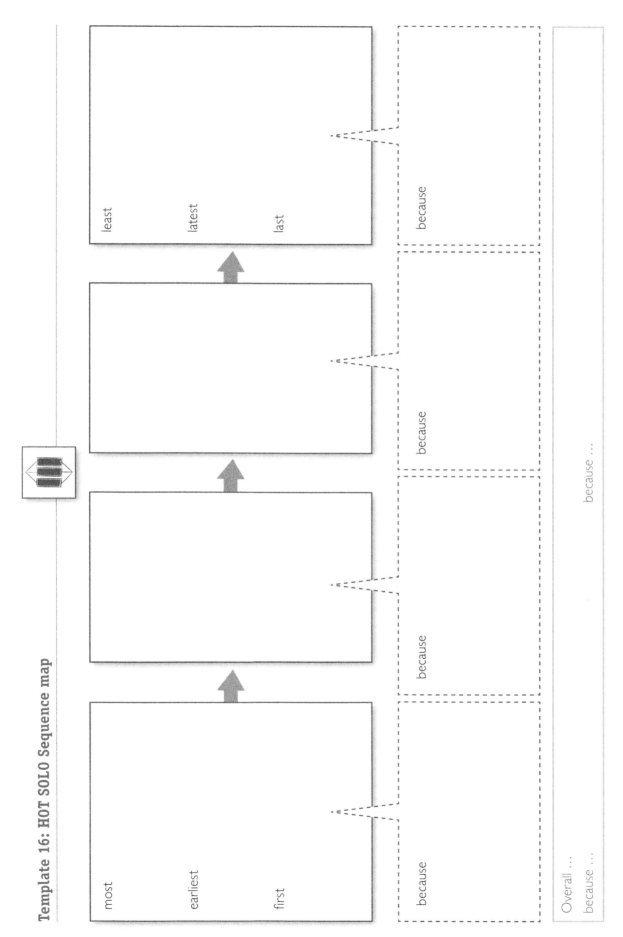

most

earliest

first

least

latest

last

because

because

because

because

Overall …

because …

because …

**HOT SOLO Sequence rubric**

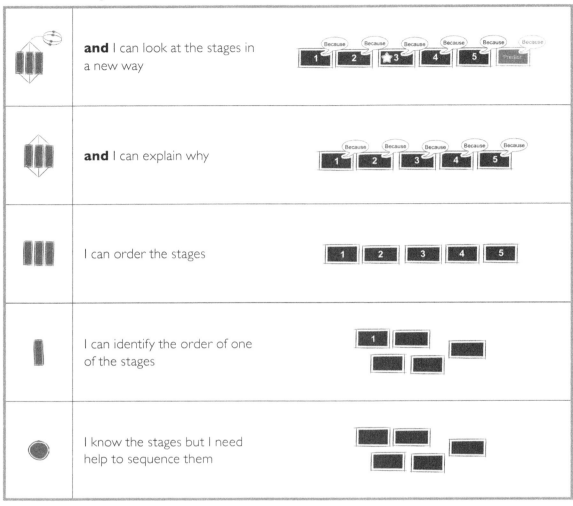

*SOLO learning log*

My sequencing statement is at a _____ SOLO level outcome because ...




My next step is to ...

## HOT SOLO Classify map and self assessment rubric

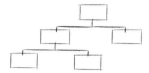

*Classify – Which of these things go together?*

**What are these resources for?**

You can use the HOT SOLO Classify map and self assessment rubric to clarify understandings by categorising or grouping ideas on the basis of similarities, shared qualities or characteristics.

**How do I use them?**

1. Align the HOT SOLO Classify map and self assessment rubric with the identified learning intention. For example, "We are learning to classify [content] [context]."

2. Group the ideas or objects on the basis of observed similarities.

3. Make subgroups within each group.

4. Arrange these groups and subgroups into a hierarchical tree structure.

5. Draw connections between the categories, explaining how and why they are distinct from each other.

6. Make a generalisation about the classification. For example, "Overall ... because ... because ..."

7. Share with the students the success criteria for classifying in the HOT SOLO Classify rubric.

8. With reference to the success criteria, students create statements to categorise an idea using the target vocabulary from the completed HOT SOLO Classify map. They can write or say their classifications or present them as a series of annotated drawings. This process is iterative, meaning that students can repeat it whenever new learning occurs and thus can improve on the original classification statements.

9. Students self or peer assess their classification statements and seek teacher feedback on them.

10. Students assess their learning outcome for the identified learning intention against the SOLO levels, explain why they have chosen this level of learning outcome for their work (feedback) and suggest "where to next" steps (feed up).

11. Students record their work in a student learning log.

Template 18: HOT SOLO Classify map

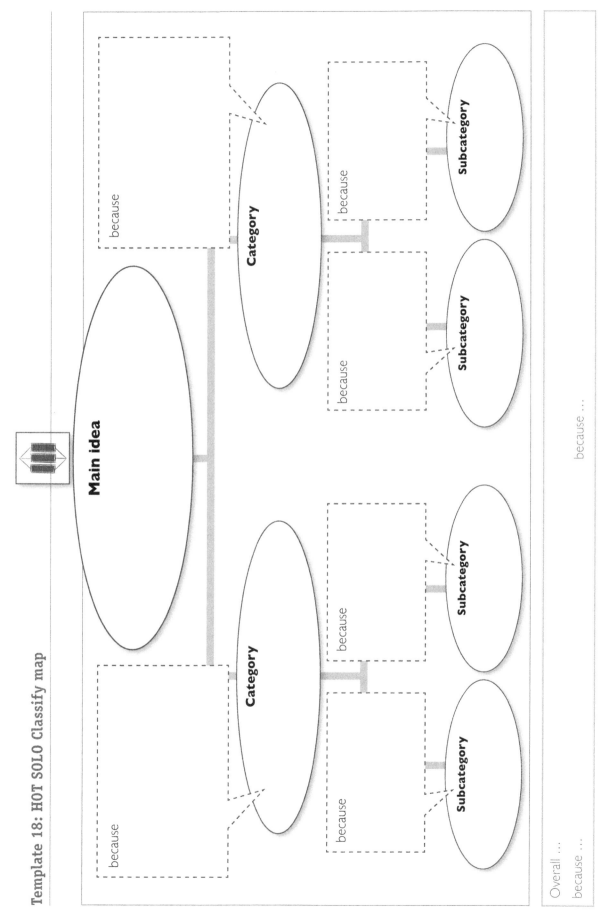

Main idea

Category

Category

because

because

Subcategory

Subcategory

because

Subcategory

Subcategory

because

because

because

Overall ...
because ...

because ...

**HOT SOLO Classify rubric**

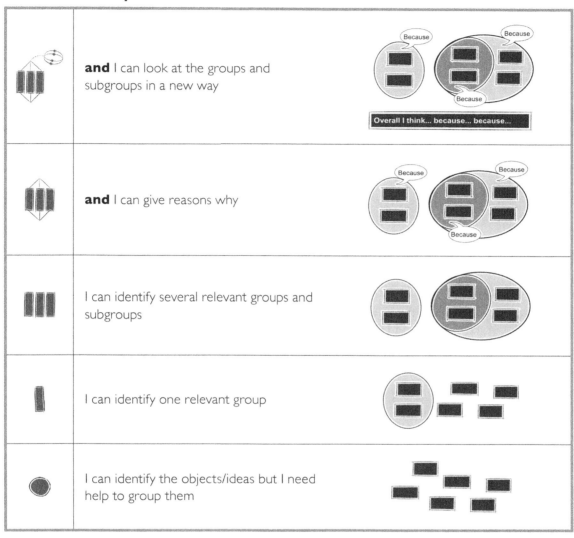

*SOLO learning log*

My classification is at a _____ SOLO level outcome because …

My next step is to …

## HOT SOLO Compare and Contrast map and self assessment rubric

*Compare and contrast – How are they similar? How are they different?*

**What are these resources for?**

You can use the HOT SOLO Compare and Contrast map and self assessment rubric to identify similarities and differences between objects or ideas.

**How do I use them?**

1. Align the effective strategy (HOT SOLO Compare and Contrast map) with the learning intention. For example, "We are learning to compare and contrast [content] [context]."

2. Identify the ideas to be compared and contrasted, [X] and [Y], and place [X] in one of the focal boxes and [Y] in the other.

3. In the boxes between the two main ideas, list similarities between them.

4. Look at each main idea separately. List the ways that [X] differs from [Y] in the boxes to the left of [X]. List the ways that [Y] differs from [X] in the boxes to right of [Y].

5. Use speech bubbles to explain these similarities and differences. For example, "They are different in this way because …"

6. Make a generalisation about the similarities and differences between the two ideas. For example, "Overall I think [X] and [Y] are more similar than they are different because … because …"

7. Share the success criteria for comparison in the HOT SOLO Compare and Contrast rubric.

8. With reference to the success criteria, students create a comparative statement using relevant similarities and differences and the target vocabulary from the completed HOT SOLO Compare and Contrast map. They can write, say or make an annotated drawing of these statements. This process is iterative, meaning that students can repeat it whenever new learning occurs and thus they can improve on the original comparative statements.

9. Students self or peer assess their comparative statements and seek teacher feedback on them.

10. Students assess their learning outcome for the identified learning intention against the SOLO levels, explain why they have chosen this level of learning outcome for their work (feedback) and suggest "where to next" steps (feed up).

11. Students record their work in a student learning log.

**Template 20: HOT SOLO Compare and Contrast map**

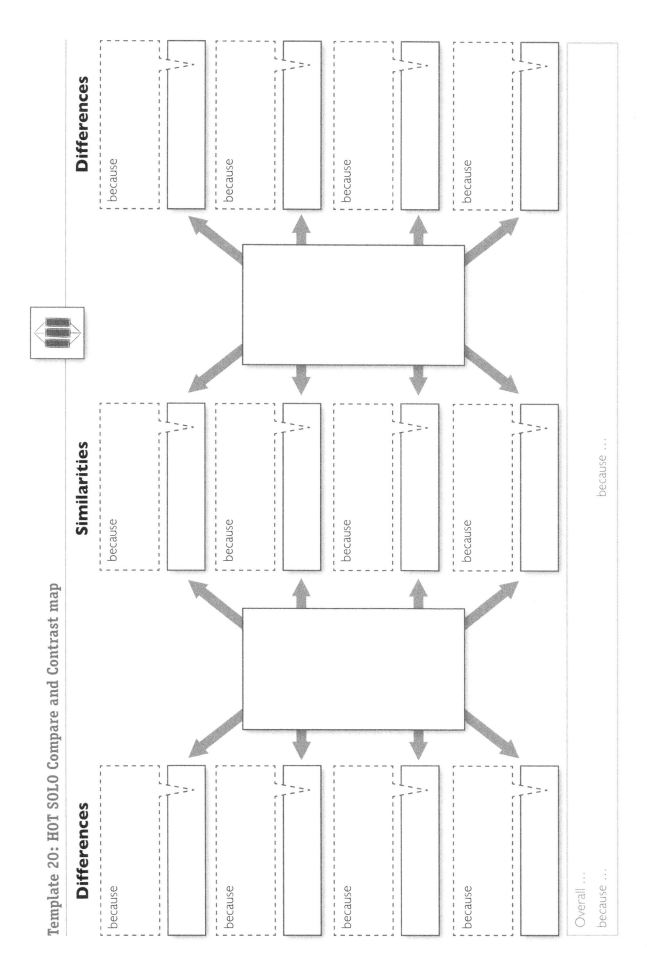

**HOT SOLO Compare and Contrast rubric**

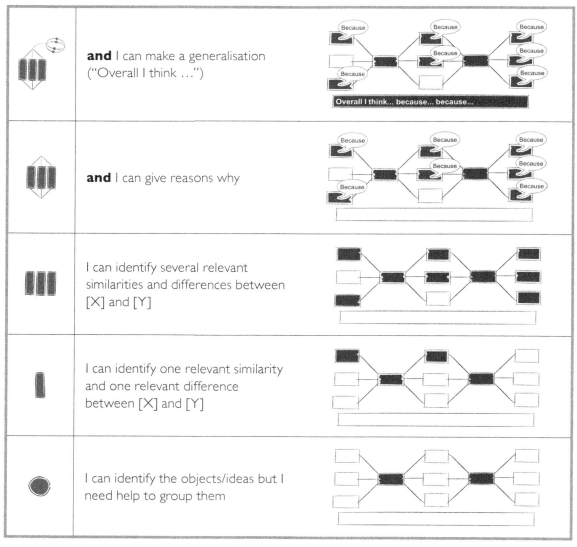

| | |
|---|---|
| | **and** I can make a generalisation ("Overall I think …") |
| | **and** I can give reasons why |
| | I can identify several relevant similarities and differences between [X] and [Y] |
| | I can identify one relevant similarity and one relevant difference between [X] and [Y] |
| | I can identify the objects/ideas but I need help to group them |

*SOLO learning log*

My comparison is at a _____ SOLO level outcome because …

My next step is to …

### HOT SOLO Cause and Effect map and self assessment rubric

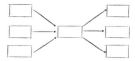

*Explain cause and effect – Why did it happen? What happened as a result?*

**What are these resources for?**

You can use the HOT Cause and Effect map and self assessment rubric to clarify the causes and consequences of an event or outcome.

**How do I use them?**

1. Align the HOT SOLO Cause and Effect map and self assessment rubric with the identified learning intention. For example, "We are learning to explain causes of [content] [context]."

2. Place the event in the centre box. It may be represented by text, a drawing, a photograph, a video or an extract from a newspaper.

3. List possible causes of the event in the boxes on the left.

4. List possible consequences/effects of the event in the boxes on the right. Note students may create a temporal sequence of short-, medium- and long-term causes and effects.

5. Place a speech bubble next to each cause and consequence and explain why it is a cause or consequence. For example, "This is a cause/effect because …"

6. Make a generalisation about the causes and/or consequences of the event. For example, "Overall I think … because … because …"

7. Share with the students the success criteria for causal explanation in the HOT SOLO Cause and Effect rubric.

8. With reference to the success criteria, students create a causal explanation statement using relevant causes and/or effects and the target vocabulary from the completed HOT SOLO Cause and Effect map. They may write or say these statements or convey them through an annotated drawing. This process is iterative, meaning that students can repeat it whenever new learning occurs and thus can improve on the original causal explanation statements.

9. Students self or peer assess their causal explanations and seek teacher feedback on them.

10. Students assess their learning outcome for the identified learning intention against the SOLO levels, explain why they have chosen this level of learning outcome for their work (feedback) and suggest "where to next" steps (feed up).

11. Students record their work in a student learning log.

# Template 22: HOT SOLO Cause and Effect map

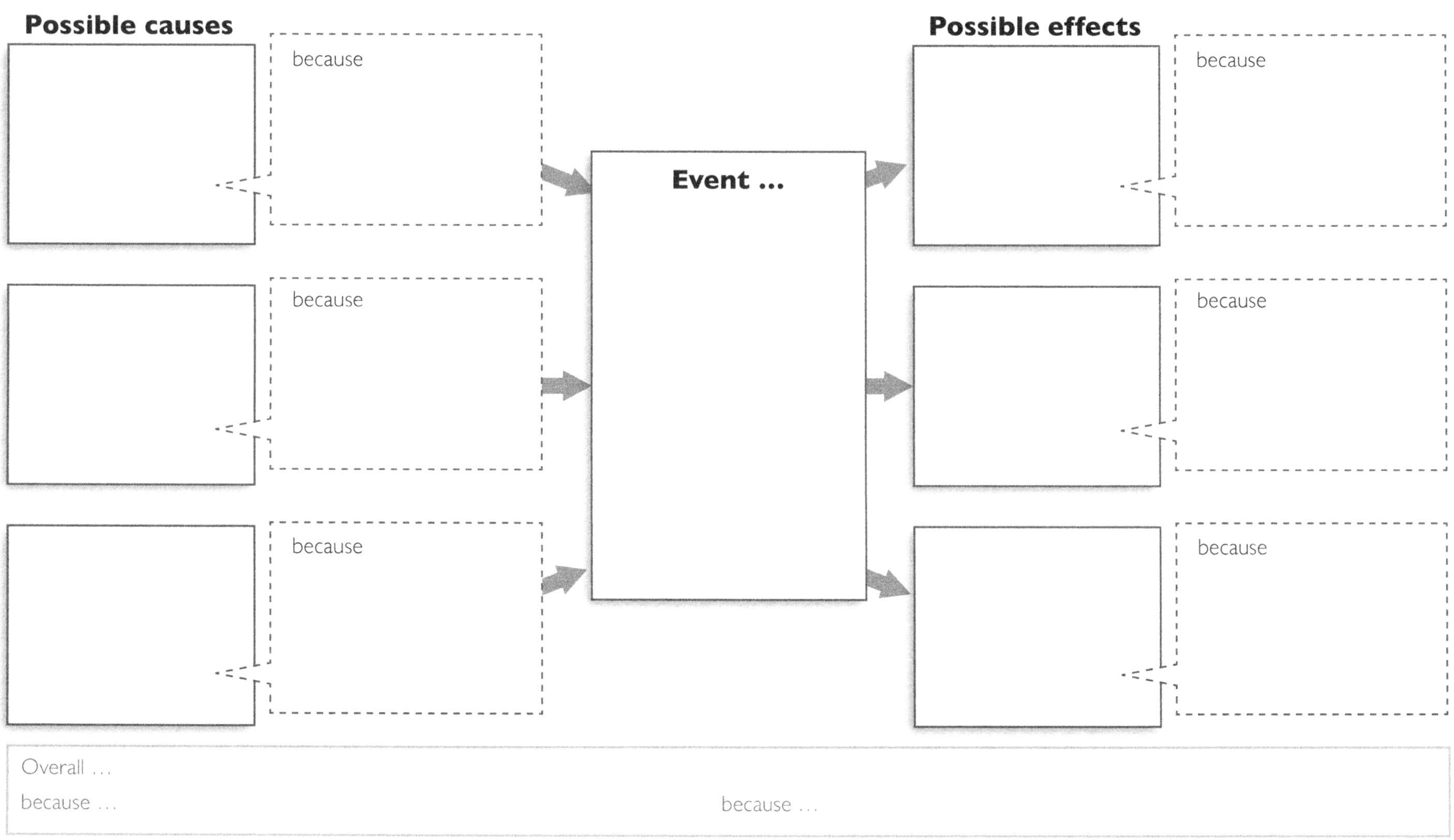

## Possible causes

**Possible effects**

because

because

because

because

because

because

Event ...

because ...

Overall ...
because ...

**HOT SOLO Cause and Effect rubric**

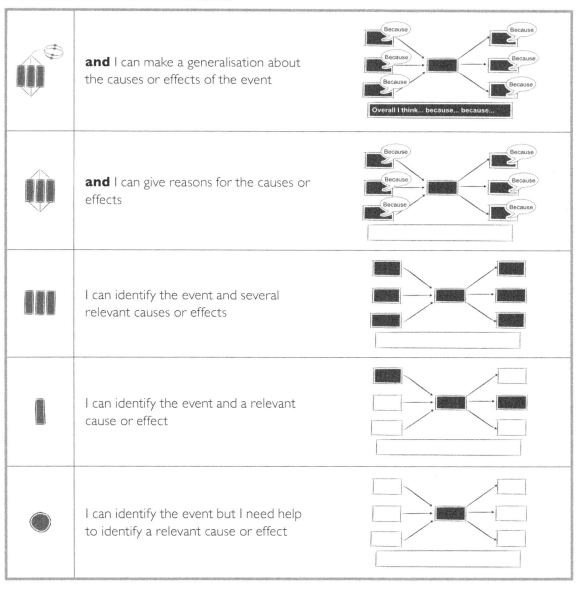

*SOLO learning log*

My causal explanation is at a _____ SOLO level outcome because ...

My next step is to ...

## HOT SOLO Analyse map and self assessment rubric

*Analyse – What are the parts and how do they work?*

**What are these resources for?**

You can use the HOT SOLO Analyse (part–whole) map and self assessment rubric to analyse an object (or an idea) by identifying the constituent parts and by determining the purpose and thus the importance of each part to the whole.

**How do I use them?**

1. Align the HOT SOLO Analyse map and self assessment rubric with the identified learning intention. For example, "We are learning to analyse [content] [context]."

2. Identify the idea or object to be analysed and place it in the left-hand box on the map.

3. List the relevant parts of the whole in the second column of boxes. These parts can be represented in a range of ways, such as text, images, photos and/or drawings.

4. Taking each part in turn, explain what would happen to the whole if that part were missing or damaged. Record all possibilities in the third column of boxes.

5. In the final column of boxes, make a generalisation about the purpose/function of each part to the whole based on the explanations. For example, "Overall … because … because …"

6. Evaluate the respective contributions of the parts to the function of the whole.

7. Under the map, make a generalisation about the relevant parts and the whole. For example, "Overall I think … because … because …"

8. Share with the students the success criteria for analysis in the HOT SOLO Analyse rubric.

9. With reference to the success criteria, students create an analysis statement using relevant parts and the target vocabulary from the completed HOT SOLO Analyse map. They may write or say these statements or convey them through an annotated drawing. This process is iterative, meaning that students can repeat it whenever new learning occurs and thus can improve on the original analysis.

10. Students self or peer assess their analysis and seek teacher feedback on them.

11. Students assess their learning outcome for the identified learning intention against the SOLO levels, explain why they have chosen this level of learning outcome for their work (feedback) and suggest "where to next" steps (feed up).

12. Students record their work in a student learning log.

Template 24: HOT SOLO Analyse map

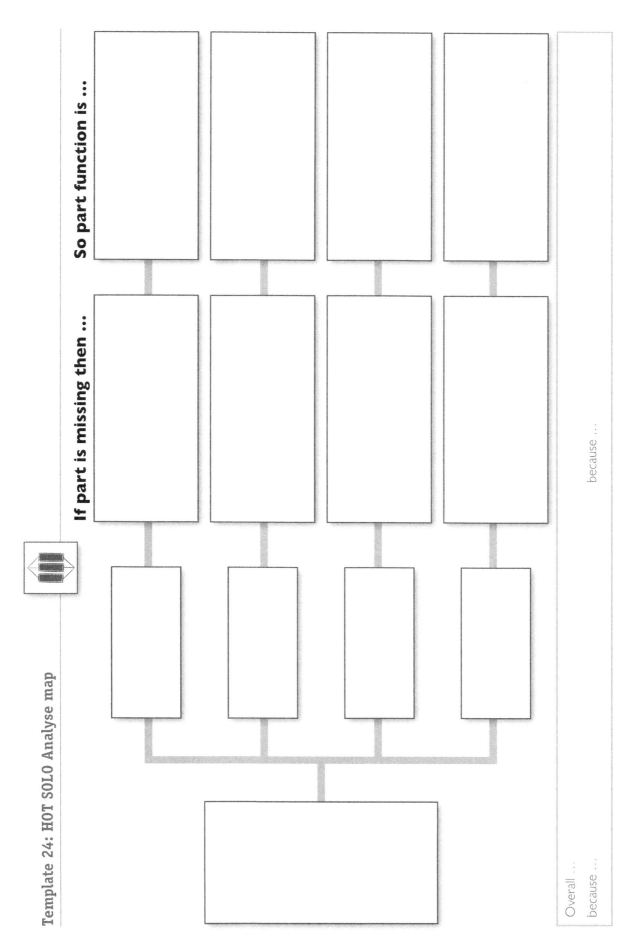

**If part is missing then …**

**So part function is …**

Overall …

because ….

because …

**HOT SOLO Analyse rubric**

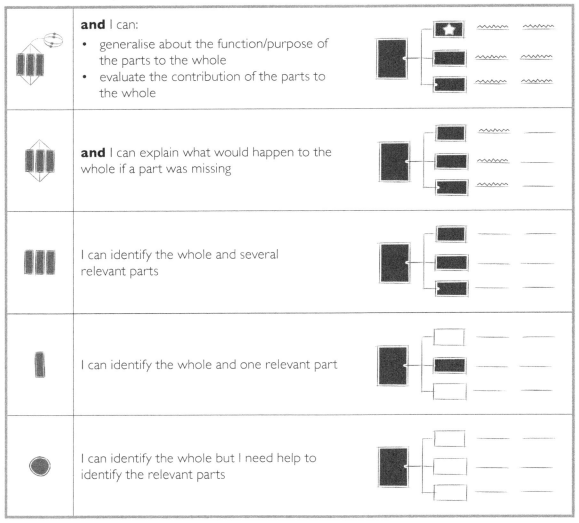

| | **and** I can:<br>• generalise about the function/purpose of the parts to the whole<br>• evaluate the contribution of the parts to the whole | |
| --- | --- | --- |
| | **and** I can explain what would happen to the whole if a part was missing | |
| | I can identify the whole and several relevant parts | |
| | I can identify the whole and one relevant part | |
| | I can identify the whole but I need help to identify the relevant parts | |

*SOLO learning log*

My analysis is at a _____ SOLO level outcome because …

My next step is to …

## HOT SOLO Analogy map and self assessment rubric

*Form an analogy – A is to B as C is to what?*

### What are these resources for?

You can use the HOT SOLO Analogy map and self assessment rubric to find similarities between two objects that are normally not alike in structure.

### How do I use it?

1. Align the HOT SOLO Analogy map and assessment rubric with the learning intention. For example, "We are learning to form an analogy for [content] [context]."

2. Choose an object and place it as object A in the bottom left box on the map. The object may be text, a photograph or an image (as can object B – see Step 6 below).

3. List any attributes that describe object A in the same box.

4. Choose one attribute and place it on the map in the top left box.

5. Brainstorm other objects – especially quirky and unusual objects – that share a similar attribute.

6. Choose one object from the brainstorm, place it as object B in the bottom right box and write the significant attribute in the top right box.

7. Under the map, explain the relational factor. For example, "A is like B in regard to …"

8. Share with the students the success criteria for analogy in the HOT SOLO Analogy rubric.

9. With reference to the success criteria, the students create an analogy using the completed HOT SOLO Analogy map. They may write or say the analogy or convey it through an annotated drawing. This process is iterative, meaning that students can repeat it whenever new learning occurs and thus can improve on their original analogy.

10. Students self or peer assess their analogies and seek teacher feedback on them.

11. Students assess their learning outcome for the identified learning intention against the SOLO levels, explain why they have chosen this level of learning outcome for their work (feedback) and suggest "where to next" steps (feed up).

12. Students record their work in a student learning log.

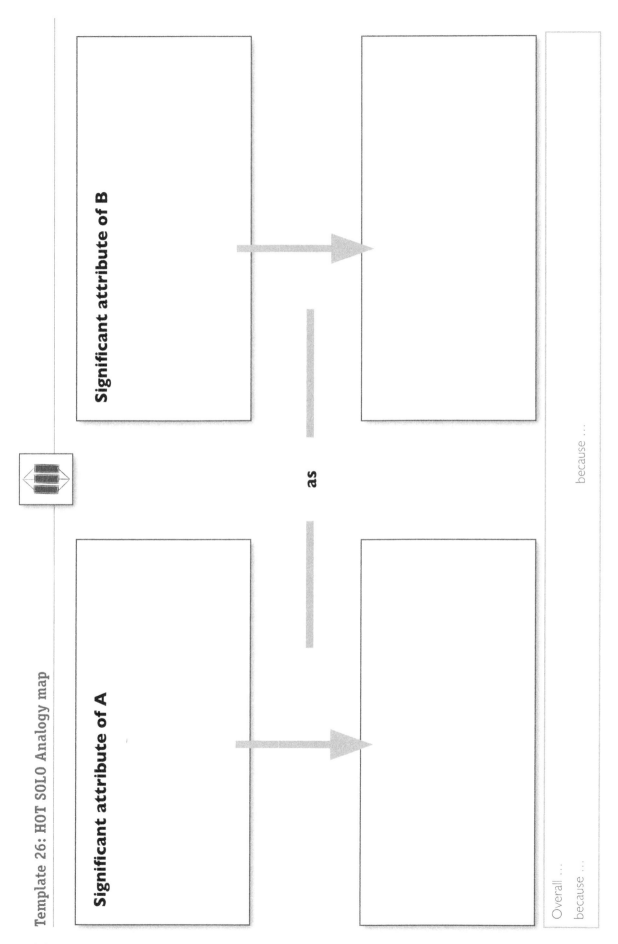

Significant attribute of A

Significant attribute of B

as

Overall ....
because ....

because ....

**HOT SOLO Analogy rubric**

| | | |
|---|---|---|
| | **and** I can form an analogy | |
| | **and** I can explain how A is like B in regard to … | |
| | **and** I can describe significant attributes of them | |
| | I can define A and B | |
| | I need help to form an analogy between A and B | |

*SOLO learning log*

My analogy is at a _____ SOLO level outcome because …

My next step is to …

# Extended abstract HOT SOLO maps

## HOT SOLO Generalise map and self assessment rubric

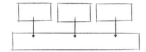

*Generalise – Overall I think … because … because …*

**What are these resources for?**

You can use the HOT SOLO Generalise map and self assessment rubric to back up the reliability and validity of a claim.

**How do I use them?**

1. Align the HOT SOLO Generalise map and self assessment rubric with the identified learning intention. For example, "We are learning to make a generalisation about [content] [context]."

2. Make a generalisation/claim, or identify a claim in the editorial section of a local paper (print) or reader comments (online).

3. Clarify the meaning of the generalisation/claim.

4. Provide reasons to support the generalisation. For example, after the first "because …", explain why the claim is reliable.

5. Provide evidence/grounds to support your reasons. For example, after the second "because", explain why this reason is valid.

6. Evaluate the generalisation.

7. Share the success criteria for making a generalisation in the HOT SOLO Generalise rubric.

8. With reference to the success criteria, students create a generalisation statement using the completed HOT SOLO Generalise map. They may write or say the generalisation or convey it through an annotated drawing. This process is iterative, meaning that it can be repeated whenever new learning occurs and thus can improve on the original generalisation.

9. Students self or peer assess their generalisations and seek teacher feedback on them.

10. Students assess their learning outcome for the identified learning intention against the SOLO levels, explain why they have chosen this level of learning outcome for their work (feedback) and suggest "where to next" steps (feed up).

11. Students record their work in a student learning log.

Template 28: HOT SOLO Generalise map

**Generalisation**

**Explain** Support generalisation with explanation (reliability)

**Example** Support explanation with evidence/examples (validity)

**Evaluate generalisation** (accept/reject/uncertain)

Overall ....
because ....

because ....

**HOT SOLO Generalise rubric**

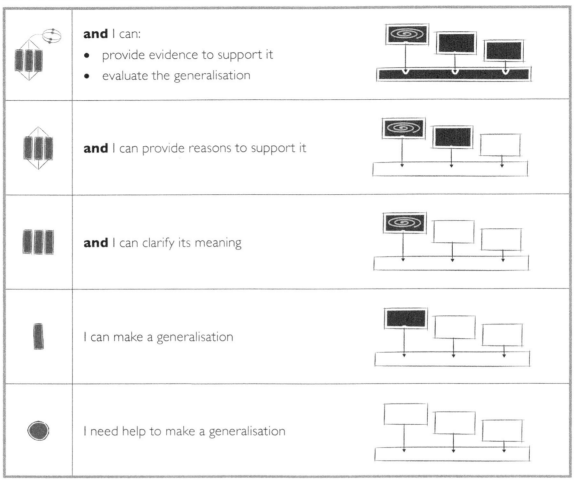

*SOLO learning log*

My generalisation is at a _____ SOLO level outcome because ...



My next step is to ...

## HOT SOLO Predict map and self assessment rubric

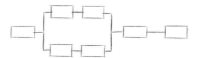

*Predict – What happens next?*

### What are these resources for?

You can use the HOT SOLO Predict map and self assessment rubric to evaluate possible outcomes before selecting one as a prediction that is likely to be realised.

### How do I use them?

1. Align the HOT SOLO Predict map and self assessment rubric with the identified learning intention. For example, "We are learning to make a prediction about [content] [context]."

2. Identify several possible outcomes.

3. Select the most likely outcome.

4. Imagine possible evidence to support the outcome, including possible information sources.

5. Imagine possible evidence to reject the outcome, including possible information sources.

6. Find actual evidence and explain why it supports or rejects the ideas about possible evidence.

7. Use the evidence to judge the likeliness of the possible outcome and decide if you will use it as your prediction.

8. Formulate a prediction or repeat the process with another possible outcome.

9. Share with the students the success criteria for making a prediction in the HOT SOLO Predict rubric.

10. With reference to the success criteria, create a prediction statement using the completed HOT SOLO Predict map. The students can write or say their prediction or convey it in an annotated drawing. This process is iterative, meaning that students can repeat it whenever new learning occurs and thus can improve on the original prediction.

11. Students self or peer assess their prediction and seek teacher feedback on it.

12. Students assess their learning outcome for the identified learning intention against the SOLO levels, explain why they have chosen this level of learning outcome for their work (feedback) and suggest "where to next" steps (feed up).

13. Students record their work in a student learning log.

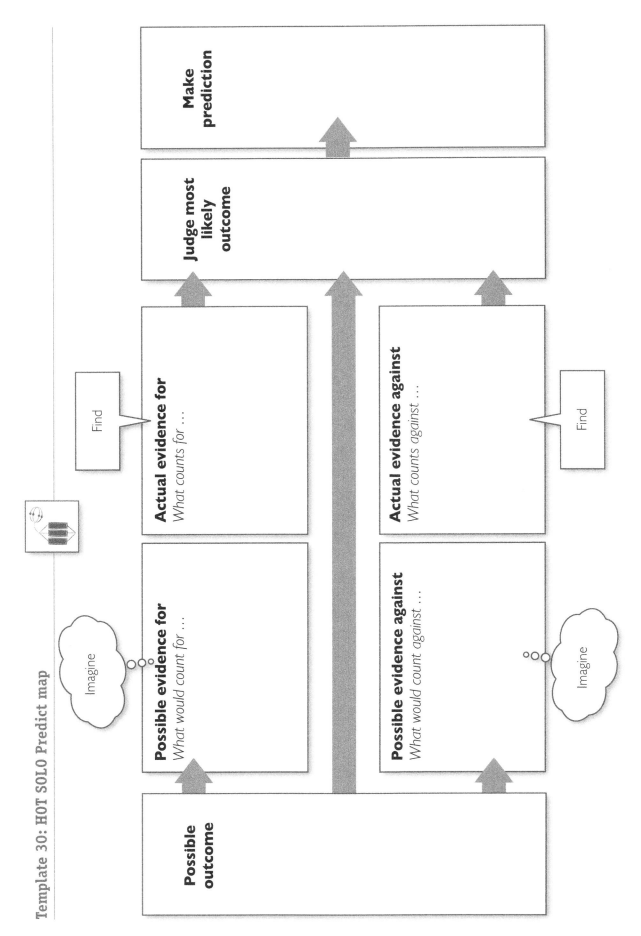

Make prediction

Judge most likely outcome

Find

**Actual evidence for**
*What counts for …*

Find

**Actual evidence against**
*What counts against …*

Imagine

**Possible evidence for**
*What would count for …*

Imagine

**Possible evidence against**
*What would count against …*

**Possible outcome**

**HOT SOLO Predict rubric**

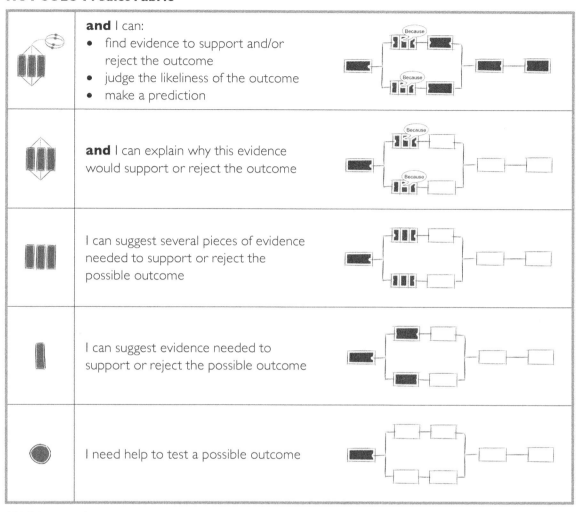

| | **and** I can:<br>• find evidence to support and/or reject the outcome<br>• judge the likeliness of the outcome<br>• make a prediction | |
| --- | --- | --- |
| | **and** I can explain why this evidence would support or reject the outcome | |
| | I can suggest several pieces of evidence needed to support or reject the possible outcome | |
| | I can suggest evidence needed to support or reject the possible outcome | |
| | I need help to test a possible outcome | |

*SOLO learning log*

My prediction is at a _____ SOLO level outcome because …

My next step is to …

### HOT SOLO Evaluate map and self assessment rubric

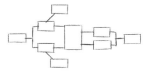

*Evaluate – What is best?*

**What are these resources for?**

You can use the HOT SOLO Evaluate map and self assessment rubric to judge ideas and outcomes.

**How do I use them?**

1. Align the HOT SOLO Evaluate map and self assessment rubric with the identified learning intention. For example, "We are learning to evaluate [content] [context]."

2. Make a contestable claim in the top box.

3. List reasons to support the claim and formulate objections against it underneath the claim.

4. For each reason and each objection, make a supporting statement explaining why the reason supports the claim or the objection refutes the claim (a "because" statement).

5. Identify grounds and/or evidence for each reason/objection and each "because" statement.

6. Judge the strengths and weaknesses of the overall reasons for the claim.

7. Judge the strengths and weaknesses of the overall objections to the claim.

8. At the bottom of the map, make an evaluation of the claim based on the reasons and objections.

9. Share with the students the success criteria for evaluation in the HOT SOLO Evaluate rubric.

10. With reference to the success criteria, students create an evaluation statement using the completed HOT SOLO Evaluate map. They may write or say their evaluation or convey it through an annotated drawing. This process is iterative, meaning that students can repeat it whenever new learning occurs and thus can improve on the original evaluation.

11. Students self or peer assess their evaluation and seek teacher feedback on it.

12. Students assess their learning outcome for the identified learning intention against the SOLO levels, explain why they have chosen this level of learning outcome for their work (feedback) and suggest "where to next" steps (feed up).

13. Students record their work in a student learning log.

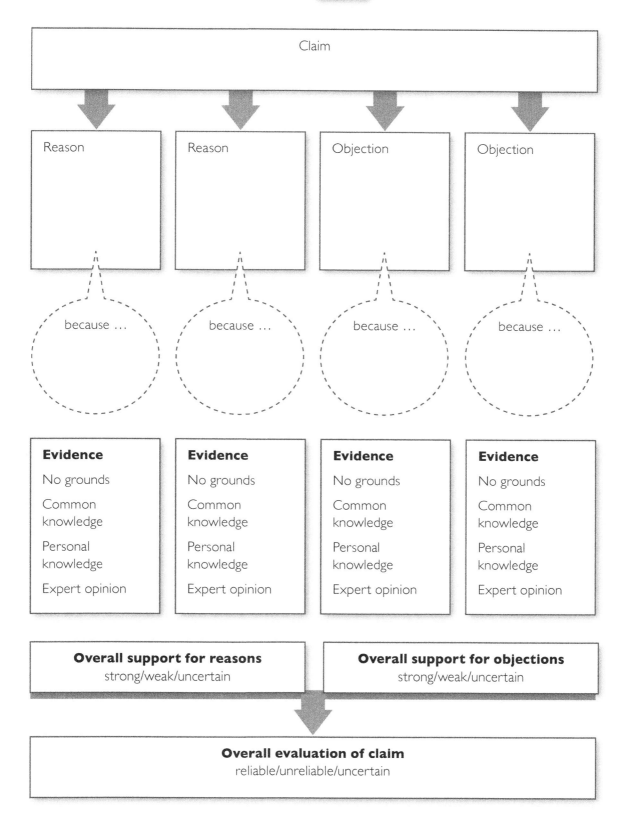

## HOT SOLO Evaluate rubric

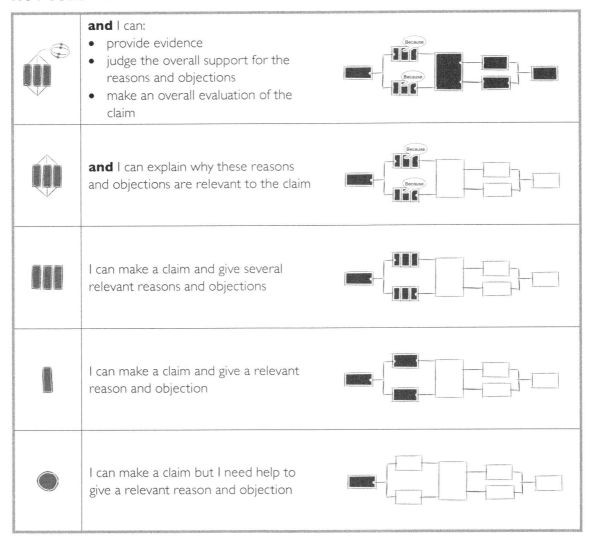

| | | |
|---|---|---|
| | **and** I can:<br>• provide evidence<br>• judge the overall support for the reasons and objections<br>• make an overall evaluation of the claim | |
| | **and** I can explain why these reasons and objections are relevant to the claim | |
| | I can make a claim and give several relevant reasons and objections | |
| | I can make a claim and give a relevant reason and objection | |
| | I can make a claim but I need help to give a relevant reason and objection | |

*SOLO learning log*

My evaluation is at a _____ SOLO level outcome because …


My next step is to …

# 4. Where to next?

The next step in the learning process with SOLO Taxonomy is to plan learning experiences and assessments to align with SOLO-coded learning intentions. *SOLO Taxonomy: Planning learning experiences*, the second book in this series, explores how to use SOLO Taxonomy to meet the New Zealand Curriculum principles of high expectations, coherence and inclusion, learn to learn and future focus. The book provides templates and examples showing how to use HOT SOLO maps and self assessment rubrics as effective strategies for learning.

# References

Anderson, L.W., & Krathwohl, D.R. (2001). *A Taxonomy for Learning, Teaching and Assessing: A revision of Bloom's taxonomy of educational objectives.* New York: Addison Wesley Longman.

Biggs, J. (1999). *Teaching for Quality Learning at University.* Buckingham: Buckingham Open University Press.

Biggs, J.B., & Collis, K.F. (1982). *Evaluating the Quality of Learning: The SOLO taxonomy.* New York: Academic Press.

Biggs, J., & Tang, C. (2007). *Teaching for Quality Learning at University. What the student does* (3rd ed). Berkshire: Society for Research into Higher Education & Open University Press.

Bloom, B.S. (1965). *Taxonomy of Educational Objectives.* London: Longman.

Hattie, J.A.C., & Brown, G.T.L. (2004). *Cognitive Processes in asTTle: The SOLO taxonomy.* asTTle Technical Report 43. University of Auckland/Ministry of Education

Hattie, J.A.C. (2011). *Visible Learning: A synthesis of over 800 meta-analyses relating to achievement.* London and New York: Routledge, Taylor and Francis Group.

Hook, P. (2006). A thinking curriculum. *Curriculum Matters* 2: 81–104.

Hook, P. (in press). Teaching & learning: Tales from the ampersand. In L. Rowan & C. Bigum (eds), *Future Proofing Education: Transformative approaches to new technologies and student diversity in futures oriented classrooms.* Springer.

Ministry of Education. (2007). *The New Zealand Curriculum for English-medium Teaching and Learning in Years 1–13.* Wellington: Learning Media.

# Index of templates

HOT learning log – three-level assessment task (Template 6)   *19*

HOT SOLO Analogy map (Template 26)   *52*

HOT SOLO Analyse map (Template 24)   *49*

HOT SOLO Cause and Effect map (Template 22)   *46*

HOT SOLO Classify map (Template 18)   *40*

HOT SOLO Compare and Contrast map (Template 20)   *43*

HOT SOLO Define map (Template 12)   *31*

HOT SOLO Describe map (Template 14)   *34*

HOT SOLO Evaluate map (Template 32)   *61*

HOT SOLO Generalise map (Template 28)   *55*

HOT SOLO Predict map (Template 30)   *58*

HOT SOLO Sequence map (Template 16)   *37*

Learning verbs and literacy outcomes (Template 11)   *27*

Overview of HOT SOLO maps paired with their learning verbs (Template 10)   *26*

Overview of the key ingredients in achieving a learning outcome (Template 7)   *21*

Putting the effective strategy (HOT SOLO map) within a broader framework (Template 8)   *23*

Self assessment rubric (co-constructed) for SOLO declarative knowledge (Template 3)   *9*

Self assessment rubric (co-constructed) for SOLO functioning knowledge (Template 2)   *8*

Self assessment rubric for HOT SOLO Analogy map (Template 27)   *53*

Self assessment rubric for HOT SOLO Analyse map (Template 25)   *50*

Self assessment rubric for HOT SOLO Cause and Effect map (Template 23)   *47*

Self assessment rubric for HOT SOLO Classify map (Template 19)   *41*

Self assessment rubric for HOT SOLO Compare and Contrast map (Template 21)   *44*

Self assessment rubric for HOT SOLO Define map (Template 13)   *32*

Self assessment rubric for HOT SOLO Describe map (Template 15)   *35*

Self assessment rubric for HOT SOLO Evaluate map (Template 33)   *62*

Self assessment rubric for HOT SOLO Generalise map (Template 29)   *56*

Self assessment rubric for HOT SOLO Predict map (Template 31)   *59*

Self assessment rubric for HOT SOLO Sequence map (Template 17)   *38*

SOLO constructive alignment (Template 5)   *17*

SOLO hand signals (Template 4)   *12*

SOLO levels and symbols (Template 1)   *7*

Target vocabulary for HOT SOLO maps (Template 9)   *24–26*

Lightning Source UK Ltd.
Milton Keynes UK
UKOW06f1433110614

233217UK00004B/26/P